Camperva _____ ____

Outback Australia, with a camper trailer, three kids and a dog.*

By John Perrier

* P.S. There was no dog.

Title and Copyright notice

"Campervan Kama Sutra"
By John Perrier

Published by JP Publishing Australia
Copyright 2015 John Perrier
ISBN 978-0-9875694-5-5
Travel/Humour

Also available as an E-Book
ISBN 978-0-9875694-6-2

Please see the end of the book for

More titles from this author
Ways to connect with us.

Contents

Prologue

I turned the ignition key.

Nothing.

I turned it again, a little more desperately this time. Again, nothing. Not even a tiny click. The engine was dead.

Outside of the Jackaroo, the river was lapping at the wheel arches, trickling muddy water in through the door cracks. The rear vision mirror reflected the mortified faces of my three children. In the passenger seat, my wife's taut expression was even more concerning.

"It will be fine, everybody," I lied. "It's probably just water shorting out the battery." Then I rolled up my shorts in a futile attempt to keep them dry, waded through the waist-deep water to the boot, and rummaged through a pile of soggy camping gear for the tow rope - the only piece of equipment that could help us now.

Then I led my family to the river's edge to wait. We hadn't seen another car all morning. This could take a while….

*

When I had the notion to take my family on a tour around outback Australia in a camper-trailer, it had seemed like a dandy idea. I shopped the concept around to family and friends to gauge their opinion of such an undertaking, and was met by an overwhelmingly positive response.

You'll have a great time. The kids will learn more on a trip like that than they'd learn at school. What an opportunity!

These types of optimistic sentiments came from everyone except one person: my wife Kath. She had a few (dozen) misgivings, among which was: "What if the car breaks down, and we're stuck in the middle of nowhere, and nobody is around to rescue us?"

When she had raised this issue, I had done what any experienced husband does when faced with concerns of such a clearly hypothetical nature. I ignored it.

For the last two months of our trip my policy of targeted ignorance had served me well. I assumed that Kath had forgotten ever raising such doubts. But I could tell by her stony silence as we sat by that riverbank - staring at our partially submerged car, waiting and hoping that help would eventually arrive - that unfortunately, she hadn't.

Even worse, it was her birthday.

Ouch.

Chapter One: Preparations

Earlier that year...

The flight from Brisbane to Perth took nearly six hours. Sitting for that long on a seat designed for one buttock gives you ample time to reflect on how damn big this country is. As we flew 10 kilometres above the massive heart of Australia, I was humbled by the thought that this great land was ours to discover: the wonderful coastline, rugged centre, fascinating history and unique flora and fauna. So upon landing, to best prepare the kids for the enlightening three-month journey that lay ahead of them, Kath and I took them for their first educational outing: *The Lucky Shag* Pub.

We'll come back to *The Lucky Shag* shortly. But first, before we even step off that plane, you should know at least something about the people you're joining on this three month journey. After all, if you're going to accompany us from Perth to Darwin, and then south through the red centre, then you'd best get to know your travel companions.

As you may have extrapolated from the little car incident in the Prologue, my wife Kath was not thrilled with the idea of living car-and-tent fashion for a quarter of a year. Her preferred *modus operandi* for a good vacation would be a couple of weeks in a seven-star hotel (six star hotels are sooo 1990s), during which we'd dine thrice daily in expensive restaurants and take high tea in our breaks. This holiday would also include numerous poolside cocktail bars at which they served drinks other than beer or bourbon. No, gentlemen, I don't get it either.

I have never actually checked with Kath, but her fantasy holiday would, er, probably not include me. No, ladies, I don't get that one either.

So when I first proffered the notion that we take our kids on a three-month tour of hot, dusty outback Australia in a camper trailer, it would be fair to say that she did not immediately leap at the opportunity. Following the ensuing discussions, in which she realised that her objections to our grand adventure were simply being ignored (including the one about the car breaking down in the middle of nowhere), we finally agreed, by a voting margin of one-all, that we would undertake an epic family voyage west of the black stump.

Timing was important. Within two years, our eldest daughter Caitlin would graduate to high school. Caitlin is not only cute but also very bright, but perhaps not quite bright enough to catch up on three months of lost work in the rough-and-tumble of senior school. Far easier to miss the time in primary school; the trip would more than compensate for 60 missed show-and-tells.

Our middle son, Lachie, was in a similar situation. He, too, would soon be graduating to a senior school, albeit into grade five. He simply could not afford the time off lest someone pinch his spot on the footy team.

Our youngest offspring, Jacob, was now big enough and sufficiently robust at seven years old to cope with life on the road, including being dragged on arduous bushwalks and being made to swim across shark-infested bays by his gung-ho father.

We therefore had a narrow window of opportunity that lay between Jacob being too young, and the other kids being too advanced in their schooling and sporting objectives. There wasn't a nanosecond to waste.

So began the preparation and planning. Naturally, being a bloke, this was almost as much fun for me as the trip itself. I scoured guide books and maps, and spoke to anyone who had so much as flown over north-western Australia. Countless hours were spent on the internet visiting exotic travel sites, reading travel blogs, looking at travel photos and getting travel advice. After a month of dedicated research, my brain was so full of The Kimberley that I could feel its red dust seeping out of my ears. It was time for action.

First, I calmly deduced, we would need a new vehicle. Although we already had a fine car, my earlier research suggested doubts as to whether my 1979 Mazda RX-7 two door hatchback sports car would manage the trip. I was especially concerned about its ability to tow the trailer, and to navigate the river crossings in far north Western Australia.

Just as my reservations were emerging, "Rex" blew a radiator on the way home from netball one night to seal his fate of retirement from active service. I made the heartbreaking decision to trade him in. I dropped Rex off to the dealership with the same sense of foreboding as when one takes an aging cat with a broken leg to the vet. I can tearfully recall the sad look on Rex's little car face as his pop-up headlights lowered for the last time.

Into the void appeared a second hand 2002 Holden Jackaroo. I would like to say that we gave the car a cool family nickname but in truth it was simply known as "The Jackaroo". Then again, had the real name of the model been, say, a Holden "Jack", then we may well have extended the moniker to "The Jackaroo" anyway, so it's like the car came with a pre-ordained nickname.

The Jackaroo's previous owners were a lovely old couple who had already taken it on a road trip through the Northern Territory. They had wired up the Jackeroo with a dual-battery system that powered a 12-volt fridge in the boot. When we purchased the car from them, they generously included the fridge and batteries into the bargain. Furthermore, they charitably offered us a free loan of their fully-functioning camper trailer, including a heap of camping gear – chairs, tables, lamps, and yes, even a kitchen sink. They threw in some fishing gear that they thought they would no longer use. Very generous indeed were this lovely old couple.

Yes, Mum and Dad were always very good to me.

Gradually, over the next couple of months, I accumulated, accrued, begged and borrowed more camping gear. It would also be fair to say that I pilfered a bit as well off unsuspecting friends. I don't like using the word *stole*; it is so harsh, and reeks of wrongdoing. *Pilfered* is a much softer term that more accurately represents the act of borrowing some disused tent poles out of a mate's garage and not returning them for a couple of years. Well, I intend on returning them soon, anyway.

In arranging our inventory, I hoped to cover every reasonable contingency. We had to be self-sufficient. Car spare parts were mandatory, as was rescue gear – tow ropes, a good car jack, two spare tyres and the like - as well as a comprehensive tool kit. We also had water containers of various sizes, two spare fuel jerry cans, and a 20HP generator. The trailer had a battery on board in addition to the spares in the Jackaroo's boot, so a solar panel for trickle recharging was added to the inventory.

A six by three metre pop-up tent would serve for shelter alongside the camper trailer, and two first aid kits were meticulously prepared. I ordered a custom-made solid fibreglass esky – not one of those crappy plastic ones – to keep foodstuffs cool, liberating fridge space for extra beer.

Bedding was next on the list. The trailer had a large comfortable mattress *in situ* for Kath and me, but even though our kids are pretty tough, I didn't think that they'd appreciate sleeping on the cold hard floor of the camper-trailer for three months. And I certainly did not intend to share our matrimonial mattress with three squirming, worming offspring. The mum-and-dad-only part of the marriage was a problem that I had yet to address adequately, but I knew that the first part of the solution was procuring separate sleeping arrangements for the kiddies. My little brother solved this dilemma by loaning me three portable bunk beds, assuring me that they were a breeze to erect.

All of this gear steadily accumulated on the garage floor. By the time I added pots and pans, food storage drawers, kitchenware, various collapsible cupboards, two tables, five chairs, the same number of sleeping bags, three boogie boards and assorted sporting gear into the mix, our double garage was crammed from one wall to the other. A mate even offered me a metal detector – *who knows when it could come in handy*, he insisted – which I respectfully declined.

I did some quick mathematics. Actually, I lie — Kath did the mathematics for me. She's a maths teacher, and thinks that multiplication is fun. She calculated that our garage had a floor area of about 50 square metres, the contents of which had to be somehow crammed into a trailer measuring 2 metres by 3 metres. I was sure Kath had made a computational error somewhere, but no matter how many times she repeated the arithmetic, the answer was obvious: it wasn't going to fit.

By the time I added a box of family games, fishing equipment (including four rods and my growing collection of brightly coloured lures) and two large containers full of wet suits and snorkelling gear, the pile had migrated into the laundry and was heading up the stairs toward the kitchen. Yet we still had to pack personal gear — clothes, pillows and the like — as well as last minute items like perishable food. And a carton of beer had to be slotted in there somewhere too.

I tried trimming the pile, but to no avail. Everything seemed vital. Sure, we could omit some non-essential items like toothbrushes, but that was hardly going to solve our problem. I asked Kath to help me cull, but she ended up *adding* a computer, a small make-up case, some nice wine glasses and a beach umbrella.

My mate Andy came to the rescue. During his family's camping phase - this stage was now defunct as his wealthy brother had bought a beach house - he had purchased a very large, solid roof rack cage. Just the thing for a long trip. He no longer used it and agreed to loan it to me for the duration of the trip. (I'll have it back to you soon, Andy, I promise. Along with those tent poles that mysteriously vanished from your garage.) Sure, we still had to cram a lot of stuff into a few tiny spaces, but the roof rack was bound to help. Heck, I'd pile everything up Beverly Hillbillies style if I had to.

Unfortunately the legs of the cage wouldn't fit directly onto the Jackeroo, so I headed to the local auto shop to buy some commercial roof racks to which I could then bolt the tray. I was served by a pimply faced 19-year-old whose chin was adorned with a pathetic, wispy excuse for a goatee. He walked me down a distant aisle to where the roof racks were displayed.

"Mate, I reckon the *Pro Racks* are your best bet, mate," he assured me with blokey confidence.

"How much weight can a Pro Rack hold?" I enquired, estimating that I had at least 70-80 kg of gear and a 50-odd kg tray to hold aloft.

"Oh mate, Pro racks, they hold heaps, mate. Yeah, heaps."

I fixed him with the steely penetration of my bullshit detecting gaze until he began to wilt. He added another "maaate" to break his unease. I thanked him for his knowledgeable contribution to my decision making process and scanned the package's fine print. I wasn't inspired by the "Made in China" label, but discovered that they were rated to 55kg each.

Heaps... Maaaaate....

To ensure I had sufficient load capacity, I bought two pairs of racks, and installed three of the struts to the top of the Jackaroo. My little brother pilfered the spare. What purpose he has for a single roof rack I cannot imagine.

A few hours and 28 bleeding knuckles later (yes, you have 28 knuckles - count them if you don't believe me) the roof rack was sitting proudly atop the Jackaroo. Yet when looking upon the expansive pile of equipment on the garage floor I was still enveloped by a sense of hopelessness. It seemed impossible to fit even a fraction of the gear into just a small trailer, a roof rack, and a car boot. However, I was helped in this task by a most unlikely skill.

I was a teenager in the 1980s, so I grew up when computer games were in their infancy. Our computers had none of the fast movement, surround sound and dizzying hi-resolution graphics that are standard today. Instead we had clunky movement controlled by a pubic-hair-filled keyboard (how did that stuff get in there?), 16-colour screens (256 if you were prepared to pay big dollars for the WOW! factor) and chunky screen pixels that I swear, from memory, were the size of sugar cubes.

Because of their inherent limitations, computer games of the period were gawky and crude. One that I played was called *Tetris*. For those uninitiated technophobes out there, or those readers born after 1990 who have never heard of Tetris, the premise was simple. Computer-generated shapes would descend from the top of the screen, and by manoeuvring and rotating them with the keyboard arrows as they fell, you had to position them so that they built a solid wall. The shapes were initially simple – squares and rectangles – but grew more irregular as the game progressed. Any gaps in your resultant wall would cause points to be deducted, and you lost your turn if you didn't slot the shape into the wall in time.

At school, while pretending to do work at computer club, I would secretly play Tetris. After a few weeks of practice I could guide a 15-sided rectangular block into a slot at a glance, then rotate an upside-down, even more confabulated shape into a non-descript gap. My proud mastery of Tetris was bought to an abrupt halt by my teacher, Mr. Allen, who loudly informed me that I was wasting my time playing such a foolish game as it would never help me with anything in real life.

Well, Mr Allen would be proud - or perhaps disgusted, I'm not sure which – to observe that three decades later I had clearly transferred my Tetris skills to good use. Over the next two days, I twisted, turned and manoeuvred that camping gear on the garage floor into the most unlikely of gaps. No matter how difficult or awkward the size or shape of the item I somehow managed to fit it neatly into a slot, just like a real life Tetris blocks. My nerdy game-playing days had empowered me with a Ph.D. in Packing.

Hour by hour the garage pile diminished, admittedly with much trial and error, and associated swearing and cussing. By the end of the second day, I had done it. Everything was packed. Sure, we were chock-a-block, but we were ready to go!

There was just one small problem. It was April. We weren't due to leave until June.

Not wanting the waste this monumental packing achievement, I hastily convened a weekend camping trip with my mate Tod and his family. We headed to a spot called Lake Monduren, about five hours north of our home in Brisbane. We were going to test our new camping set-up and give the fishing gear a run as well. I wanted to get amongst the barramundi up north, and I had heard that Lake Monduren was full of them.

Apparently.

Tod and I spent three days casting our lines endlessly into that lake without so much as a single hit. We tried every fishing option in the book: hard lures, soft plastics, thin leaders, longer casts, quicker retrieves, etcetera etcetera bloody etcetera. We tried fishing calmly, and thence swearing vociferously. We tried fishing soberly (for a little while) and then we tried it drunk. Then even drunker. But all without luck. I estimate that we cast-and-retrieved about 5000 times each over that long weekend and returned with nothing but sore arms and sunburn.

How was the camping? How were the organisation, the set up, and the pack up? In a word, amateurish.

Worst of all were the bunk beds that my little brother had promised me would be oh-so-easy to assemble. Bereft of instructions, it took me fully an hour to piece together the struts, cross supports, uprights and many other nameless bits to form what look like the framework for a bunk bed. Then I had to virtually disassemble the same in order to fit the mattress slings.

Other bits and pieces also took too long to erect or dismantle. Sure, that little gadget that the camping store salesman had assured me would 'only take five minutes to set up' probably did take only five minutes. But when you multiplied half a dozen bits and pieces – a camp bin, clothes drying hoist, storage shelves, fishing rod holders etc – by five minutes each, you quickly accrued half an hour of fiddling. Add to that another half an hour to disassemble them all and you're wasting a lot of precious drinking time.

I had hoped to complete our camp set-up and pack-up in about 30 minutes each. I acknowledged that this would take some practice, but our first effort at Lake Monduren took over three hours. At this rate we would be spending our entire trip doing little more than assembling and disassembling bloody camp beds and the like.

I spent the next few weeks discarding these 'time saving devices' and replacing them with even simpler alternatives. The bunk beds were the first to go, replaced by simple thin foam mattresses to which I had affixed a layer of waterproof matting. Set up time: ten seconds. Pack up time: ten seconds. Time already saved: an hour or so per day. The storage shelves, which required rudimentary construction, were replaced by hanging flexible baskets. And so on. Fiddle time was the enemy. By the time we tested our gear during a second practice camp we had reduced our set up to about an hour. Not bad, and that would (and did) improve with practice.

Satisfied that we were now ready for adventure, I booked a logistics company to transport both car and trailer to Perth, 5000 km away on the other side of the continent. We had no inclination to start our journey with a dull, flat drive across the featureless Nullarbor Plain. We wanted to save dull, flat drives across featureless plains for later in the trip.

The logistics company rep. duly arrived, and completed a detailed condition report and inventory of the car and trailer. Every tiny scratch, bump and nick was dutifully recorded. This filled me with confidence that the logistics company were professionals, and that they would take good care of our new home – our car and camper trailer – en route to Perth.

On June 1, we boarded the plane. We were carrying bags packed full of items that *somebody* had decided were absolute necessities, despite three month's preparation and two practice camping trips having been successfully completed without them. I don't wish to cast aspersions on any particular member of the family, so I won't mention *her* name. (It wasn't Caitlin.)

By the way, do not ever trust the scales that the airlines use to weigh your luggage. They weighed our largest bag on the pretext that it looked too heavy. (It wasn't.) As a matter of interest, I jumped on the scale myself. Before the check-in lady shooed me off, the scale registered 96.9 kg. I can assure you that this reading is inaccurate, as it precisely matched my weight as measured on our bathroom scales at home, which I am pretty sure read overly-heavy by about 10 kg.

We passed the five hour flight peering out the window, and reflecting on how damn big this country is. As we flew 10 kilometres above the massive heart of Australia, I was humbled by the thought that this great land was ours to discover: the wonderful coastline, rugged centre….

Actually, that is a complete lie. I spent the time playing a game with Caitlin called "my favourite (x) is…" in which (x) is a food, drink, colour, superhero or brand of bourbon, whatever you fancy. The other person then has to guess what, for example, your favourite colour is. Riveting fun. I stumped Caity for hours on the bourbon question. She couldn't think of *any*. Honestly, the ignorance of the young people these days. All she had to do was look at the steadily-escalating pile of cans on our seat tray to figure it out.

Before we knew it, we had touched down at Perth airport. The holiday was now officially underway. *The Lucky Shag* Pub was only hours away.

Chapter Two: Perth

Sad when the first call of the trip is to your lawyer.

When we picked up our trailer in Perth, I noticed that the transport company had completely cracked the aluminium frame that supported the front stone guard. Not just bent it, or dinted it; they had shattered it completely through – an act that would require great force, complete negligence, or, more likely, a combination of both.

I pointed this out to the yard bloke immediately, assuming they had a simple and coherent system for righting such mishaps. He directed me to the manager, to whom I duly demonstrated the trailer's injury. He glanced at the damage, and then turned to me with an expression that somehow combined an amused grin with "as if I give a shit", and "get off my property now".

I insisted that things were clearly not as they had been when the trailer left our house in Brisbane, and miraculously produced a non-lost receipt of the condition report to prove it. He retaliated by providing a copy of the contract I had signed, and noting Section 6, subsection iii, paragraph 4, clause XXIV, line 23, which permitted them to attack my car and/or trailer with a pick axe if they so desired, without penalty or compensation.

"Sort of makes this detailed condition report superfluous then, doesn't it?" Unfortunately this cretin did not know what *superfluous* meant, so I was dismissed with a grunt.

I called head office to enquire as to their policy for repairing such indignities. The lady on the other end of the telephone line replied in a voice that conveyed the tone of an amused grin with "as if I give a shit", and "get off my phone now". I guess you can be smug once an unsuspecting – nay, trusting – individual has signed a contract with exonerating clauses like Section 6, subsection iii, paragraph 4, clause XXIV, line 23.

After attempting to appeal to this woman's reasonable side for a few more minutes, I sensed the hopelessness of the debate. Her tone hadn't changed one iota – I could tell that she still had that irritating grin on her face. So I turned my sarcasm indicator up to overdrive, thanked her *very much* for her help, and hung up before she could annoy me any further.

My next call was to my aforementioned lawyer, Brian. He informed me that despite Section 6, subsection iii, paragraph 4, clause XXIV, line 23 in the contract, I probably still had a case for them to repair the damage. All I had to do was fax him copies of the contract, the condition report, photographs and description of the damage, and a log of all conversations or communications that I had entered into with any members of the logistics company, including times, dates and outcomes.

That seemed like an awful lot of work – heck, I was officially on holidays. So I decided to drop the whole incident out of my mind and spent the remainder of our conversation simply making Brian jealous of the fact that I was going on holidays for three months.

I strapped the stone guard together with some old plastic pipe, insulation tape and cable ties, and used some spare rope to stop it from flapping in the wind.

The repair kit had come in handy before we'd driven even a centimetre.

After checking into our hotel in downtown Perth, we ventured out for lunch at a local café to kick off our tour in style. We kept walking, passing by a dozen trendy cafes with sumptuous sounding menus. Unfortunately, they were all closed. As were the next dozen. Inexplicably, the streets were deserted. We eventually found a 24-hour-7-day kebab shop, and placed our order. By the look of the other customers hunched around the tables, the kebabery was also a clandestine meeting place for the local paedophile network. We'll have take-away, thanks.

We grabbed our food and bolted. Apart from the paedophiles, we did not pass another person. Nor did we see another shop of any sort that was open. I concede it was Sunday afternoon, but downtown Perth seemed like a ghost town.

This thought was reinforced later that afternoon when we headed out for a wonderfully aimless walk to explore the city and, in particular, the mighty Swan River that coursed its way through its centre. We quickly encountered a beautiful big park that stretched for about a kilometre between the river and the city. It was a sunny afternoon, and the river was glinting, glimmering, and glitzing in the light, yet there was not another person in sight. The emptiness of such a fine park so near to the city centre was unsettling.

It took me couple of days to realise why the park was so empty. It is because the whole city of Perth is full of parks. Hundreds of them. There are so many that they virtually have one each. I guess the person who was assigned this particular park on this particular Sunday afternoon was having a sickie.

We continued our amble, thankful for the chance to stretch our legs after the long flight. With an uncanny sense of instinct, our route led us directly toward The Lucky Shag pub.

The pub was situated in a mini-boardwalk area along the Swan River. By now it was close enough to five o'clock (it was three o'clock) to settle in for a few pre-dinner drinks. Kath had a Margaret River Chardonnay, while I settled for a few schooners of the local Pale Ale, with the obligatory Red Lemonade for the kids. After a dinner of very light, crispy fish-and-chips (or am I just judging generously in comparison to the sludge that passed itself off as 'lamb shanks' on the plane flight?) we headed home for an early night.

*

The next morning we threw ourselves head first into the tourist scene with a mini-bus tour of the nearby Swan Valley wine district. While not as illustrious as her southern big sister Margaret River, which produces some of Australia's —nay, the world's – finest wines, the Swan district had plenty to offer the discerning (or thirsty) tourist.

The best thing about the Swan was its location: it was only a 20-minute drive from Perth's city centre. The Swan's central town is historic Guilford, which is famous for a number of "firsts": the first pub built in Western Australia, the first domestic house built in Australia that is still used as such, and Lilac Hill, a local cricket ground at which they play the first match on each English tour.

However, Kath and I were far more interested in another "first": our first glass of wine.

We didn't have to wait long. The Swan is packed with wineries, of which we visited five. At each stop, we started with the whites (after which Kath sensibly stopped), thence to the reds, and finally the ports and other fortified wines. At a rough guess, I consumed about 45 teeny glasses of wine that day. Keep in mind that I consider spitting out a perfectly good mouthful of free alcohol a crime comparable to genocide. Needless to say, I was feeling very comfortable by the end of the trip.

The kids entertained themselves admirably, and were aided in this task by a 20-year-old computer geek from Adelaide called Michael. I'm not sure how much drinking experience young Michael had acquired since becoming of legal age, but I quickly sensed that it was not a lot. This turned out to be a good thing, as he was one of those drunks who gets a dopey look on his face, smiles a lot, and loves a chat, however inane. The kids quickly sensed his hopelessly inebriated state and closed in for the kill. Even Jake, who will barely offer you a word until he's known you for a year, was giving him heaps by the third winery. They passed the entire last hour in this witty repartee, with Michael blissfully unaware that he was having the mickey taken out of him by a bunch of pre-teens. He'll make a great father one day.

The kids' real reward came at the end of the tour when we visited a chocolate factory. The attached retail outlet had free samples – three huge bowls, filled with dark, milk and white chocolate buds respectively. The shop was very busy, and a sizeable queue had formed in front of the freebies. The idea was that you quickly sampled a couple of buds from each bowl and then moved on. But not our boys. Lachie and Jake set up camp at those bowls for the entire 20 minutes, despite the queue of people steadily filing past them. They certainly set a very high standard for our "cheapskate traveller's creed" that would last the rest of the trip.

During our game of "What's your favourite (x)…" on the plane the previous day, I discovered that Caitlin's favourite food was nougat. So I was overjoyed on her behalf to discover that the Swan Valley tour also included a nougat tasting. Caity responded in a fashion that made her dad, and her brothers, very proud: she unashamedly tasted all six nougat samples, and followed up by purchasing a large pack of nougat all-sorts to fill any gaps left after the chocolate factory. We didn't need much dinner that night.

*

Buoyed by our successful first day, we were even braver on the second, aiming for a self-driven triple treat of Perth's tourist hot spots: the West Australian Aquarium, the Perth Mint, and Fremantle City, including a tour of the old jail.

The aquarium was fine. I was a little annoyed that the lady at the door wouldn't let me bring in my hand fishing line and a few lures — the old stickler. (Just kidding, folks.) One great feature of the aquarium was that the exhibits were designed according to geographical sections of the West Australian coastline. Given that we were about to travel virtually the entire length of the coast, this was a more-than-useful education. Despite the ecological value of the displays, my mind simply could not help sizing up every fish I saw for a frying pan.

Next stop after lunch was the old Perth Mint, which is now a museum of gold prospecting and processing. The exhibits contained lots of touristy things – watching a gold bar being poured, models of the largest gold nuggets ever found etcetera. Did you know that the top 25 largest ever nuggets were all found in Australia? You could also weigh yourself in gold - I am worth $3,400,000 at current prices. That's nearly what I am worth in petrol.

At another station you could lift up a real 3 kg bar of gold. It was amazingly heavy for its size- it must have weighed at least 10 kilograms!

To cap off the day we caught a train down to the seaside town of Fremantle, known universally as *Freo*, and started with a tour of the old jail. It was very worthwhile. The spartan conditions, harsh punishments and cold, cruel nature of the place were made even more stark by knowing that the facility only ceased operations in 1991. For example, the original cell size was tiny – barely 1.2 by 2.1 metres. That's about the size a modern public toilet cubicle, but for the inmates of Freo Jail it was Home Sweet Home. The architect must have been the same bloke who designed the plane seats.

Basins were installed in each cell, but because s-bends hadn't been invented in the 1850s, foul smells would leech back up the pipes. Poor plumbing also meant constant damp. There were no toilets, so prisoners had to use a bucket that they kept - well, in theory they kept it in the corner of their room, but with 1.2 by 2.1 metres in which to work, rest and play, I'm not sure where they kept it. One can only imagine the smells and bacteria. Unbelievably, the bucket-as-a-toilet situation persisted until the prison's close only a couple of decades ago.

We also saw, and were temporarily locked in, the solitary confinement rooms. They were cramped, dank, and completely dark. There was virtually no sound, no telephones, and no video game music. These cells were supposed to be a tough, feared punishment, but personally I found it a relaxing change of pace. I asked the guard if he could lock me in there for a few hours, but he refused. Stickler.

The final, and eeriest, part of the tour was the execution room, complete with trap door, death chair, and, of course, a big thick cord entwined into a hangman's noose. The chair was obviously inert, and I daresay the trapdoor by itself wouldn't scare anyone. But adding that noose to the setting stunned us onlookers into eerie silence. Some people were so overcome that they had to leave the room. How compelling, that something as simple as a knotted rope could project such all-consuming emotions.

Did the kids get any value out of the jail tour? Let's just say that when we returned to the car and I used the old-dad-staple-line of "put on your seatbelts because if the policeman catches you without it on *you will go to jail*" they buckled up in record time.

The concluding part of our day was a walk along the Fremantle foreshore. My stated intention for this evening amble was to soak up the sights and sounds of this vibrant market area, and for everyone to experience the hum of a maritime city as the distant sun sank over the ocean. In reality, I secretly steered us towards the Little Creatures beer brewery, whereupon the family feasted upon a fine assortment of pizza while I drank my way through the card.

*

The next morning, Wednesday, heralded our last day in Perth. We took a 90-minute boat cruise out to "Rotto". Rotto is really named "Rottnest Island", but the locals all call it Rotto, so we did too. Rotto's vibe is very much enhanced by its vehicle ban. The only way to cover any distance was by bicycle.

Our bikes had somehow survived the Nullabor crossing under the expert guidance of our transport company – yes, the same idiots who had busted our trailer - so off we rode. A casual peddle over the undulating mounds of Rotto's coastline sounded like a jolly old way to spend the afternoon.

Two hours later, with our ferry departure time approaching, I puffed and heaved my way laboriously back toward the harbour area. Although my cycle had 15 gears, I hadn't changed out of first for half an hour. Four feet behind me, tethered to my bike by occy straps, were Jake and Lachie, who had long since decided that anything over 5 km was just too far to ride, and that a tow from dear old dad would be a far more agreeable way to experience Rotto's delights. Downhills were kind of fun, but uphills ... at least my quads got a decent work out. It only took me four days before I could walk down stairs again.

We just had time for a quick walk to find some quokkas. These marsupials are native and exclusive to Rottnest Island, and constitute a major tourist drawcard. They are virtually synonymous with Rotto, and feature heavily on its promotional material. The locals say the Quokkas look like cute, miniature kangaroos. To me, they looked more like fat lazy rats.

Mind you, I am not alone in this opinion. It was shared by a very brave and adventurous fellow called Willem de Vlamingh (rhymes with 'flaming'). In 1696, Bill sailed his boat from Holland, trying to find some mates that had ventured this way a few years before, and not returned. He didn't find them, but he did discover Rottnest Island. He named it Ratten-nest, meaning – how's your Dutch these days? Go on, have a guess – yes, that's right, Rat's Nest. So, in the opinion of Mr Vlamingh, the quokkas did indeed resemble rats.

Despite this very makeable mistake, Vlamingh quickly developed a high opinion of Rotto. He wrote in his journal "I had great pleasure in admiring this island, which is very attractive, and where it seems to me that nature has denied nothing to make it pleasurable beyond all islands I have ever seen." Easy for him to say; he wasn't towing two boys on pushbikes for five hours.

We were soon on the ferry, steaming our way back to Perth, very much in agreement with Billy Vlamingh. Rotto left us with the impression of a wonderful little island, with a laid-back, casual vibe.

Finally, as we leave Rotto, I have some free advice for the Island Hotel: I think a great name for one of your lounge cocktails would be a 'Vlamingh Sambucca'. *Boom tish*. Thank you.

Chapter Three: Perth to Kalbarri

Although we had already been away four days, it still felt like we were "getting ready" to go on holiday. To me, staying in a hotel in a big city felt like cheating. On day five of the trip, we finally hitched up the ol' camper trailer and headed north from Perth on Highway One. I explained to my awed children that this road – the great Highway One – went all the way around Australia, and would eventually, if we followed it without turning or deviating, lead us all the way back to Brisbane.

Half a dozen turns later, each of which was accompanied by "but Daa-aad, you said that if we followed the road without turning...," I retracted my earlier statement.

Amazingly quickly, suburban Perth gave way to West Australian countryside. Once out of the city we passed thick eucalypt forests, drove on meandering roads that coursed either up or around the hills, and frequently encountered charming little towns that dotted the highway. The land harboured many farms, and domestic animals such as cattle and sheep herded under roadside trees. It was ever-changing, with plenty to see along the way.

Put your hand up if you believed even a single word of the crap in the last paragraph. I'm not being unkind here, just truthful, when I say that virtually the entire West Australian coastline is flat and monotonous. It is a treeless scrub that stretches off seemingly infinitely in every direction. The road rarely turns, there are no hills, and the place names on the map more often represent road-house garages than towns. The earth is uniformly red ochre. There are seemingly no farms, and no farm animals. Just flat, endless scrub.

In my pre-trip imaginings of how our journey would pan out, I pictured the kids peering curiously out of the car windows as a different and exciting new world rushed by. They were going to learn about Australia, a mile at a time, through keen observation, and a series of insightful questions.

This prediction was put to bed very early in the trip when one of them asked: "Dad, what are those bushes?"

"Er, I think those low greenish ones are, um, Acacias," I guessed, "while those other green lowish ones are, er, Banksias." In truth, I made the names up, but that's not the point here. The point is: that was it. There was nothing else to look at.

For 10000 km.

I took solace in the thought that if God/Allah/Buddha/(insert-the-deity-of-your-choice) wanted children to look out of the car window and ask meaningful questions, then He/She/It/They would not have invented portable DVD players.

I have been informed that this countryside is considerably more interesting –nay, spectacular – in wildflower season. However, we were passing in winter, and only the odd hardy flower survived.

You soon got used to the open empty space. In fact, I grew to like having a permanent 360 degree vista, even if it consisted of bugger-all. I've also developed genuine pity for any outback aboriginals born with agoraphobia[1].

Our first stop in the vast expanse of WA was a town called Cervantes, which is better known as the gateway to Nambung National Park. Nambung, is, in turn, better known as *The Pinnacles*. After setting up an abbreviated camp – we only planned to stay overnight – we headed out to explore this unique countryside.

The Pinnacles desert is a Martian-type landscape formed from large upstanding limestone blocks, which rise up like red-ochre giant tombstones from the coastal sands. They are from 50 cm to three meters high; some are pointy on the top, like Indian tepees, while others are box-like. It's as if the aforementioned God/Allah/Buddha/Whoever took a gigantic box of deity-sized Lego blocks, dumped them on the floor at Cervantes, and forgot to clean them up.

We spent a pleasant hour or so circumnavigating the park via the 4 km loop track. Well, Kath, Caity and I walked. The boys ran. And climbed. And jumped off anything with a foothold, trying to prove that little boys *can* fly if they really try hard enough. Thankfully, the sand was forgiving, and they somehow managed to avoid serious injury.

We headed off early the next morning. As the road ploughed due north, the occasional glimpses of the Indian Ocean gave me an unexpected insight into the WA coastline: there is no surf. Give any east-coaster like me a map of Australia and I'll bet that he or she will look at that long jagged west coast and assume that the

---

[1] Agoraphobia – look it up for yourself, it will be funnier that way.*

* Oh, Ok, I'll tell you – it's a fear of wide open spaces. #

Jokes are never as funny when they're explained, are they?

waves roll in with the regularity of a Burleigh breaker. Not so. For 99% of its length, it is as still as a millpond.

Wait, hang on, I've never even seen a millpond, so I can't say with any authority that a millpond is always still. Let's just say the ocean was as still as a lake on a windy day. Or perhaps, more accurately, a lake on a windy day with a few choppy little waves breaking here and there. That's about how still the WA coastal seas were. Either way, whatever you compare it to, this gentle surf means that the beaches tend to be narrower and rockier than are their eastern counterparts.

I don't want to sound like a whinger, especially this early in the book, but another problem of the flat WA landscape was a lack of trees. No trees means no shade. And, more importantly: Where is a bloke to hang his hammock? This oversight by Mother Nature was a tragedy of Shakespearean proportions that I intended to remedy the next time I saw two trees within cooee of each other.

We also had not yet had a campfire, as, besides the lack of burnable materials (another symptom of a treeless society), there are "No fire" signs up everywhere. I simply could not fathom how some numb-nut bureaucrat, no doubt sitting in a distant government office, deemed that the entire western coast of Australia was ill suited to small campfires.

The chances of a bushfire out there are miniscule. Those scrubby shrubs look like they wouldn't burn on a hot day in hell - although I admit I have no knowledge or evidence with which to endorse this statement. The bushes – those Acacias and Banksias - are all so low that I reckon I could dig a serviceable firebreak with a garden trowel. Sitting around an evening camp fire is one of the simple pleasures of camping life, and to have it denied for no obvious reason was frustrating. But we nevertheless remained good camping citizens and resisted the urge to have little (petrol-assisted) evening bonfires. Our supply of roasting marshmallows remained sadly untouched.

I'm not knocking WA here – I love the place – but a word of caution: if you're planning a surfing, campfire and hammock-lying tour of the West, best consult your tour guide first.

The striking exception to the "no surf and no beaches" rule was our next stop: Kalbarri. Along this little stretch of coastline, the surf absolutely *pounds* in. I don't where the waves came from, and I don't know why they singled out Kalbarri to the apparent exclusion of the rest of the coast, but these guys were monsters.

On our first afternoon in Kalbarri, I vainly attempted to do some surf fishing. I was standing in only knee-deep water, yet the force of the waves nearly knocked me over. I refused to let the kids even get their ankles wet – I am serious here – for fear that they would be swept away. The waves were almost three metres high, and crashed down relentlessly onto reef and rock. It was only the steep slope of the beach that stopped them surging over the land like a tsunami. To think that – I am not making this up – the woman in the tourist information office had recommended this beach as the best place to take the kids boogie boarding.

Yet despite all of this power and danger, there was a rash of a dozen or so surfers ripping up the waves in turn. Ok, I admit the term "rash" is not the official

33

collective noun for surfers. The official collective noun for surfers is a "wave". This word just didn't sound right, so I made up a better one.

To me the equation for the rash of surfers was straightforward: One slip = head on rock with great force = possible death, probable concussion, or at least grim disfigurement. Maybe none of the surfers knew what "equals" meant, but I can assure you that these boys had balls.

We spent an entertaining hour on a headland just watching those young bucks ripping up and down those waves, with the setting sun highlighting the ocean spray behind them. It was most spectacular, with a very reasonable admission price of $0.00 each.

I didn't catch any fish by the way.

My pathetic knowledge of geology prohibits me from telling you authoritatively that it was the relentless pounding of those waves over the millennia that gave Kalbarri its spectacular surrounding coastline. But it's a good theory, because the local coastline is as majestic a stretch of cliffs as you will see anywhere. In places, the erosion had isolated massive columns of rock, and occasionally formed arches across to the mainland. We had giddying hike along the cliff top walk, admiring the sunshine, the bird life, and the views (which included, as luck would have it, some gorgeous Scandinavian backpackers who joined the trail just ahead of us).

Some of Kalbarri's scenery reminded me of the Twelve Apostles, famous rock formations along one of Australia's most scenic drives, the Great Ocean Road. I had visited there a decade previously while on a golfing tour with a bunch of mates. One of our party had wondered aloud how far it was to a particular rock column – one of the aforementioned Apostles. An argument broke out, and bets were placed, with estimates ranging from 50 metres up to 500 meters. Trust me, it is very difficult to estimate distances over an expanse of empty ocean.

It seemed like a futile discussion as we had no way of measuring the distance – until someone produced a set of golf clubs and a few dozen old balls. For the next 15 minutes, we took turns in hacking golf balls toward the Apostle, trying in vain to land one on the "putting green" at the top. Finally, one of my mates, Damian, who, unlike me, can actually play golf, hit the green with a lovely lofted 5–iron, giving a measurement of about 160 metres. Bets were duly settled. To this day, that golf ball is probably still up there, waiting for Damian to take his birdie putt.

I had no idea how far out it was to Kalbarri's rock formations, and unfortunately I had no golf clubs with me to find out. However, the walk was very worthwhile and very picturesque, and would have been so even if the Scandinavian backpackers had not added to the view.

*

The next day at Kalbarri gave me a permanent highlight of my bushwalking career. It was a trek on an inland section of the national park called "The Loop", an 8km walk/climb/scramble through some ruggedly handsome countryside. The gorges and cliffs didn't just take your breath away; they drew the words "Holy Christ/Allah/Buddha/(insert the deity of your choice)" involuntarily from your lips as the air escaped. Put this place on your Bucket List.

Accompanying me on this testing trek was an affable, chatty, and infinitely energetic young lad named Lachlan. The track was deemed too difficult for the women and children, but Lachie nevertheless insisted on joining me. He was tremendous. Despite the challenging terrain, long distance and fast pace, he didn't falter. Whenever I looked down to my side, there was Lachie, trotting along (and yapping) like a loyal terrier.

As a bushwalk, this track had it all: limitless views, majestic cliffs, varied topography and a nicely challenging route. The path initially traversed high ridgelines, before winding its way down into the valley, where the river provided cool relief. Excuse the cliché, but words just don't do this place justice; you'll just have to imagine the vast red cliffs, warm sunshine and peaceful tranquillity of this countryside.

Actually, ignore that bit about the peaceful tranquillity. Lachie was probably chatting at the time.

The half way turning point provided the most hair-raising moment. At this point, the track traversed along some steep rocks, about five metres above the river. By following rudimentary signposts and by carefully picking our way up and down the rock face, we slowly made our way around the bend. But then, inexplicably, the signpost pointed directly over a steep cliff face toward the river.

Had some lark moved the sign? A closer inspection revealed that, no, it was firmly *in situ*, and had not been tampered with. Yet it was undeniably pointing over the cliff. Were we supposed to jump and swim? Surely not.

Then Lachie noticed a narrow ledge, only about a foot or two wide, protruding out from the cliff. After further investigation, we concluded that the sign must have been directing us along this narrow pathway. However, the ledge had another outcrop, only a few feet above it, meaning that it was impossible to stand up, let alone walk. Further tentative inspection indicated that the ledge could *possibly* be traversed - if we crawled.

The cliff face ahead arced backward around the river bend, making it impossible to see what lay ahead. Not wanting to risk slipping on the ledge and possibly falling into the river, thereby ruining my expensive camera, I opted for the sensible option: I sent Lachie ahead to check it out.

For a few nervous minutes, my first–born son disappeared from view. By the time he yelled out, letting me know that he had reached relative safety at the other end of the outcrop, I had barely had time to finish the last of the bourbon in my hip flask.

I tentatively set off along the same path. How did it go? Let's just say that Lachie, who fits in a one-or-two-foot wide space comfortably, managed easily. His dad, who needs somewhat more space than that through which to crawl comfortably, did not find it so straightforward. Nevertheless, after snagging numerous bits of clothing and camera straps on various rocky protuberances, as well as repeatedly banging my head on the overhang, I managed to circumnavigate the "pathway" (for want of a better term) and could again return myself to an upright, two-legged pose. My only mistake was not saving some of my bourbon for after the traverse.

After this excitement, we retired to the shade of a riverbank tree for lunch and a cool drink. We then hiked the rest of the track, feeling pleased with ourselves as the cliff face steadily shallowed, gradually giving way to a simple amble along a sandy riverbed. A final climb up a steep track reunited us with Kath, Caity and Jake.

Lachie animatedly summarised our five-hour trek, extolling the virtues of the loop track and its attendant rivers, cliffs and, of course, its hair-raising cliff crawl. He breathlessly described, in detail, the rock formations we had seen, the jaw-dropping views, and the varied flora and fauna. He outlined the physical challenges of the walk, and added little details, such as the clear echoes that you could hear when yelling across the steep valleys, and the undulations of a long-since-passed riverbed floor that had been fossilised into the rocks. He didn't miss a thing.

Jake sombrely informed us that they had eaten ice cream.

The river that carved out these wonderfully harsh gorges is called the Murchison. So the next day, rather than just admire it from a mountaintop, we got amongst it. We hired a tinny, and powered our way up the river. The five horsepower engine was tremendous; it was nearly faster than rowing! After an hour or so, we had chugged our way to the base of Castle Rock, a large stone edifice that overhangs the Murchison. We waded ashore, and, for the next hour or so, we picked our way up the rock face. At the summit, we were rewarded with fine views over the whole coastal river system. Oh, and a constant feeling that the overhang on which we were standing would give way at any moment, plunging us all to our deaths.

Sorry to ruin the suspense so quickly, but the overhang held firm. On our passage back down the mountain we discovered some bones – probably ex-kangaroo - that the weather had recently unearthed. The kids were delighted – inordinately so, I felt. We carted half a dozen bones, and no doubt a few billion bacteria, back down the mountain as souvenirs.

That afternoon the kids and I went fishing. Didn't even get a nibble. I was beginning to think that I was cursed.

Chapter Four: Denham and Exmouth

The next day we upped stumps and headed north to a town called Denham. Denham is better known as the gateway to Francois Peron National Park, which is in turn better known for a small resort known as Monkey Mia. The West Australians seem to like complicated naming structures. You may be aware of the daily dolphin feeding that occurs at Monkey Mia – an experience *unique* to this area.

Unique, truly unique - along with Moreton Island, Tin Can Bay, Sea World and about a hundred other places within a day's drive of our Brisbane home. Heck, I usually see dolphins whenever I take my tinny out fishing; all they do is hang around the boat and beg for leftover bait. But hey, we were in Monkey Mia, the *world capital* of wild dolphin feeding. We just *had* to partake of this unique ritual. We duly did our part and lined up for the grand event, at which one or two tourists from the crowd of 100 or so were selected to throw a fish to a dolphin. Whoopee.

We followed this action-packed experience by attending a talk on marine life in the area. The park ranger honed in on the nasties of the surrounding reef – stonefish in particular. Apparently, not everyone who is stung by a stonefish dies, but they all wish they had. It didn't sound like a pleasant experience. We were most impressed when the ranger stuck his hand in a bucket, and pulled out a live stonefish; you just have to miss the spine on top, he proclaimed nonchalantly, as he stroked it like a pet guinea-pig. Stonefish are surely one of the ugliest, most vile creatures that ever had life breathed into it. I just hope this supervised visit is as close as I ever get to one again.

We did learn one other fact that may someday save my life. I thought I'd share it with you, so that maybe one day it may save your life. If you are stung by a stonefish, or in fact nearly any marine creature, the best treatment, by far, is hot water – as hot as you can stand. I've heard many alternative theories – douse the wound with vinegar, apply an ice pack, apply a bandage soaked in methylated spirits, etcetera – but this solution was definitely the best and quickest cure. Why?

Stonefish venom, like most marine poisons, is based on liquid protein. Think of it as similar to raw egg white. When you apply heat, it cooks the venom in the same way as when you boil an egg, rendering it inactive. So perhaps take a thermos of hot water on your next snorkelling trip – it may save you a trip to the intensive care unit at the end of the day. If not, well, at least you can have a cuppa when you come out of the water.

*

The next day we further explored the land section of the surrounding Francois Peron National Park. Our first stop was the original station homestead that was constructed about 100 years ago. We also walked ourselves through some nature displays and the old shearing sheds.

Those shearers were made of tough stuff in those days. We were visiting during winter, when the temperature was a balmy 26 degrees, and were doing nothing more physical than a gentle amble. Yet after a half-hour stroll through the shearing area we felt par-boiled. Those shearers toiled year-round in the sweltering corrugated iron sheds, wrestling cantankerous sheep in 40-degree heat. Legend has it that they cooked their evening spuds just by keeping them in their pockets all day.

The station also had a natural spa created from warm bore water, which, even though tepid, was a refreshing change. With all of the history and natural beauty surrounding them, the kids could only lie back in wonderment and awe in the quaint, historical hot tub, reflecting and quietly assimilating everything they had seen and learned….

Actually, the kids spent their time bomb-diving into the tub. Kath kept telling them to stop, while I surreptitiously scored their efforts out of ten on my fingers when she wasn't looking. The lone National Parks Officer eventually poked his head around the corner to check on the unruliness, but even he could only grin.

From the homestead, we drove 40km to the end of the peninsular to do some short hikes and soak up the beautiful scenery. Every direction held a postcard view. That red WA dirt is sure photogenic, particularly when juxtaposed with a bright blue sky, a deep blue ocean, and thick green coastal dunes.

However, this region is famous for much more than its natural beauty: Denham is world heritage listed, boasting many unique natural features that bolster its claim. First, it has over 10 000 hectares of sea grass. These undersea meadows attract thousands of dugongs to the area – about 10% of the global population.

Another effect these vast expanses of seagrass have is that they restrict the tidal flow in and out of the bay. As the water at the inner end of the bay evaporates, it leaves salt from the seawater behind. This salt gradually accumulates, meaning the inner bay becomes hypersaline – a fancy term for "very salty". Normal marine life can't survive under these conditions, with the exception of lumpy grey coral-looking stuff called *stromatolites.*

Abandoned in these waters, the Stromatolites have no predators. This lonely neighbourhood has enabled them to exist as such for a lazy, oh, three billion years. Yes, these ugly lumps of muddy coral have been around almost since the Earth was originally formed. In biological terms, the discovery of these living fossils is akin to walking into a remote valley and finding a T-Rex chasing down a Brontosaurus. They're not very exciting to look at – sort of a marine version of dried cow poo – but their ecological significance cannot be overstated. Most importantly, they haven't survived anywhere else on Earth apart from in this bay.

Stromatolites were the first complex living things on earth. They created the oxygen that you are now breathing. Without the stromatolites, the air around planet Earth would be a foul, toxic mixture of carbon dioxide, methane and many other nasty gases. So you should be very bloody grateful to them.

When you consider the vast expanses of sea grasses, 10% of the world's dugong population, the living link to our fossil past, and of course some wonderfully picturesque coastline, you can understand why this area is world heritage listed. Oh, and plus it has dolphin feeding.

It was on the trail back from the headland that we encountered what would be the first of the "Crazy Germans" on tour. But please be aware that when I say

Germans I don't precisely mean "People from Germany". Nor am I racially stereotyping. I am in reality referring to anyone whose accent I can't place, which in general is anyone from Germany, Holland, Luxembourg, Croatia, Serbia, Eastern Europe, Scandinavia or, in fact, from anywhere in Europe. Or the northern hemisphere. Occasionally a few Kiwis and South Africans even sneak into this group. Sorry, I'm just not very good with accents; they all sound German to me.

In contrast, when I say "crazy", I generally mean *crazy*.

We came across this Crazy German who had hired himself a four wheel drive, and set off through the dunes to explore the coastline. Five minutes later, as we arrived, he was bogged up to the axles in sand. He was kneeling on all fours, frantically scooping sand from below the wheels with his bare hands. We stopped to help him out.

I wanted to speak some of his native tongue to him to lighten the moment, but the only three German lines I know are "Ich liebe dich" (I love you), "Ein beer bitte" (One beer please) and "Gutes neujahr" (Happy new year), none of which seemed just right for the occasion.

 "Have you got a shovel?" I instead enquired.

"A *show-veel*?" he replied, perhaps unintentionally taking the mickey out of my Aussie accent. "Vat is diss?"

I made shovelling motions with my arms, to which he responded with a shake of his head.

"Oh well, grab your jack and we might be able to lift the car up a bit," I suggested. "Perhaps then we could put some rocks or sticks under the wheels for traction."

"A yack? Vat is diss?"

Another brief game of charades ensued, in which I effectively conveyed the notion of a car jack, only to be met by a shrug of the crazy German's shoulders.

"A tow rope?" I ventured.

"A tau raap? Vat is diss?"

Ten seconds into my third charade of the morning, I gave up. Fetching my own snatch-strap from the boot would be quicker than trying to explain it to Herr Bogged-to-his-Axles. We were soon hooked up, and after yet another game of charades in which I explained the simple mechanics of being pulled out of a bog by an elastic tow rope, our Crazy German Friend was free. We unhooked the snatch-strap, and waved him *Auf Widersehen* as he chugged off, wheels spinning madly in the soft sand.

Less than a minute later, he was bogged again. I'm not sure how he managed this feat as our hopelessly overloaded car, complete with five passengers, was skirting along the ground with relative ease.

"Did you check your tyres?" I asked him when we again went to his aid.

"Tyres? Tyres iss goot," he proclaimed, gently kicking one to prove his point.

"The pressure," I specified. "Did you lower the pressure in your tyres? It helps you to get more traction in the sand."

His blank look said more than any charade ever could. The boys and I took matters into our own hands, and, for the next five minutes, our Crazy German Friend looked on nervously as we released air from each of his tyres in turn. He was no doubt wondering what these *Verrückt Australians* were doing. Then we again towed him free, unhitched the snatch strap and waved him goodbye.

The sounds of "danke schön" had barely stopped ringing in our ears when our CGF again ground to a halt in a sand bog. Of course, in this remote region you don't mind helping out a fellow traveller in trouble, but this was getting irritating. Again, we pulled him free – this time it was mercifully charade-free - even *he* knew the routine by now. As he set himself to drive away, I glanced at his tyres to determine if we had to lower them even further. It was then that the reason he was repeatedly getting himself bogged became apparent: our CGF was still in two wheel drive!

After remedying this situation via the complex task of shifting the gear stick, we gladly waved a final goodbye to him. To summarise his preparedness for the day, our CGF had ventured (1) in an unfamiliar rented vehicle (2) into isolated, sandy dunes (3) with no shovel, (4) no tow rope, (5) without deflating his tyres, and (6) without even realising that he had to change his transmission into four wheel drive. I wonder if the rental company ever got its vehicle back?

Of course, we'd made painstaking preparations for the trip. Our gear was top notch, and I even knew how to use most of it, so those sorts of situations were never going to happen to us.

If only.

So if you're thinking "I'm sick of this guy telling me what a wonderful time he had, and how great things were, while I'm stuck here in the office stapling reports," well, I can understand your feelings. I used to work as well, you know. So, to redress the balance somewhat, let me tell you about some of the little disasters that happened about this time.

First, the roof racks, and the large luggage cage that sits upon them, fell off. There we were, happily driving along a near-deserted track through the far end of Francois Peron National Park, when without warning our roof rack cage appeared on the bonnet of the car, gaily scattering its load of boxes and crates along the sand track as it fell.

I calmly and coolly[2] surveyed the damage. It soon became apparent that one of the Pro Rack legs that supported the cage had collapsed. This break had then caused an overload, bending each of the other five supporting legs out of shape, leading to total collapse. Most of the tensioning bolts had been blown out, and all manner of brackets and bits and bobs lay scattered along the sandy track.

At this point, I would like to take you back to a certain auto shop about six months previously, at which point the early preparations for our voyage were incubating.

I was served by a pimply faced 19-year-old, his chin adorned with a pathetic excuse for a goatee. He walked me down a distant isle to where the roof racks were displayed.... "How much weight can a Pro Rack hold?" I enquired, knowing that I had 70-80 kg of gear and a 50-odd kg tray to hold aloft.

---

[2] No I wasn't.

"Oh mate, Pro racks, they hold heaps, mate. Yeah heaps."

Heaps...

Maaaaate....

This pantomime went through my mind as I watched the roof rack cage appear front and centre of my visual field.

Luckily, I am an experienced four-wheel-driver. This exact mishap occurred on a weekend camping trip that I had attended with a bunch of mates about five years before, so I knew exactly how to respond. On the previous occasion we had unintentionally, but blatantly, overloaded the roof rack with firewood, which took the sensible course of action and collapsed only a few kilometres into our trip. But we had the wherewithal to solve the problem. We simply transferred the excess firewood into the other vehicle....

Darn, I'd forgotten to pack a spare vehicle.

We wandered back along the trail, picking up bits of roof-rack and other stuff that had formerly been held inside said roof rack cage. It's not easy finding nuts and bolts on a sandy track, I can tell you. Why didn't I bring that metal detector when it was offered?

Ten minutes later, there we were: the roof rack cage was still sitting awkwardly on the bonnet, we had no functional roof rack struts with which to hold it up, and a big pile of our gear stacked neatly beside the track. What were we going to do next? I mean, you can't exactly get your roof rack cage home by throwing it up on the roof rack cage, can you? We were in the middle of a wilderness park, a long way from everywhere. The road had been bereft of any other vehicles for a few hours, so it could be a long wait for help. Even if someone did pass by, what could they possibly do to help? This was a tricky situation. I sat for a minute to think.

The only viable plan was to drive Kath and the kids back to town (a couple of hours), unpack the Jackaroo of everything but essential safety gear (half an hour) then drive back alone to this spot. Thereupon I could *probably* fit the roof rack cage and the (hopefully not stolen) remaining gear somehow into the car, before driving back to camp around six or seven hours hence. Not a delicious sounding way to end the day. Even our Crazy German Friend would be a welcome sight now.

Miraculously, another vehicle suddenly rounded the bend ahead of us. Even better, it was not our CGF. Better still, it was a Ute with an empty tray. And to top off our lucky break, the occupants were a very helpful couple who were staying near us in Denham. Problem solved.

The couple carted our roof rack tray home, and the next morning I gratefully picked it up (furnishing a carton of beer for their kindness) and set to work on the repair. Unfortunately, the local hardware store didn't have any roof racks in stock. However, the owner, a friendly fellow named Neville, directed me to an auto store in the next town, Carnarvon.

Incidentally, the kids thought Neville was hilarious. Jake had originally misheard his name, thinking that he had introduced himself as "Devil". He wondered aloud why that man had such a funny name. After that, "Devil" he became.

As I entered the Carnarvon auto shop, I only had one firm criterion for my roof rack purchase: I would never buy Pro Racks again. I was soon served by a pimply faced 19-year-old whose chin was adorned by a pathetic excuse for a goatee. *Do you have a cousin in Brisbane*? I wondered. *Or is your look company policy?*

He walked me down a distant aisle where the roof racks were displayed. This situation was feeling disconcertingly familiar, and my sense of déjà-vu was prickling far too intensely for my liking.

"Mate, I reckon Pro Racks are your best bet, mate," he said.

All I could do was resist the urge to throttle him on the spot.

"Isn't there any other brand?"

"Nope. It's Pro Racks or nothing," he replied dismissively, clearly not empathising with my plight.

And so it was that I left Carnarvon Auto Pro shop with the only product that I was determined to avoid. I made one quick detour via Devil's hardware store to pick up some extra fastening nuts and bolts and got to work, and after losing the requisite skin off all 28 knuckles, the repair was complete. My Tetris skills were called upon again (take *that*, Mr Allen!) as I re-packed the entire ensemble so that the lighter objects were now on the roof.

I am happy to report that, with *four* Pro Racks in place, the cage remained firmly above our heads for the rest of the trip. Maybe, I now wonder, it wasn't the Pro-Racks' fault after all - although that thought leaves me wondering who else I can blame.

Our 24 hours of mishaps in Denham did not end there. The next morning *someone* slammed closed the trailer tail gate, smashing the sink's water tap assembly in the process. I also busted the tip off my fishing rod, and broke the bulb on our 12-volt fluoro lamp. These incidents each required separate trips to the hardware. By this stage I was including Devil among my closest friends.

"Say gidday to Beryl for me," I said as I left Devil's store for the fourth and final time.

To make matters worse, heavy rain set in. After two days of mishaps and poor weather, we'd had enough. We packed up a day early to search for clearer skies further north.

After a couple of hours on the road, we pulled into a roadhouse for petrol. This roadhouse, like most of its ilk out here, was very spacious. It had the requisite café, gift shop, truck stop and petrol bowsers, all spread over about an acre. In that entire expanse of space, there was but one fixed pole in the ground...

...into which I backed the trailer.

I was about to remonstrate with the office attendant and ask to see the manager to complain about the ridiculous notion of cementing a low pole in the middle of a service station. How was one to foresee that some numbnut had fixed a hard steel pole in the middle of prime trailer-backing space? I was stopped by Kath who gently pointed out that the pole was, in fact, to protect the petrol bowsers. Had it not been there I probably would have caused a major explosion, or other serious petrol-related incident.

Nit picking as usual.

In my usual good-natured way, I let the incident slide without further inflammation.

Fortunately, the trailer survived unscathed. This was because the blow was cushioned by our pushbikes, which were mounted on a frame over the rear spare tyre. Two of our bikes were severely damaged in the process. Mine copped the brunt of the damage, as it was on the outside of the rack. (I secretly vowed to henceforth keep my bike on the inside of the rack; should another similar mishap occur in the future, it would be the kids' crappy cycles that copped the dents.)

I spent the next afternoon fixing Caitlin's bicycle (successful) and attempting to fix mine (failure). I was rather chuffed at my success with Caitlin's bike wheel. It had been sorely dented by the impact, and was warped completely out of shape. I tried in vain for half an hour to wrestle it straight, but the metal rim was far too strong. I was about to capitulate when I serendipitously spied a man hole in the ground that was about the same diameter as the wheel rim. By placing the wheel over the hole and having the entire family stand on its rim, our combined weight slowly forced it roughly back into shape. Chalk up a victory for the bush mechanic.

However, *my* poor old pushie was, alas, unrepairable. I left it under a roadside tree, with a "FREE" sign gaffer-taped to the handlebars. If you ever pass up Denham way, let me know if it's still there.

Bad luck usually comes in threes, so I hoped that we had now used up all of our bad luck *viz-a-viz* mechanical breakdowns. I couldn't have been more wrong.

Chapter Five: Exmouth and Ningaloo National Park

By the end of week two, we had sunk into a smooth camping groove. After waking up late and slowly – even the kids didn't murmur until 8 a.m. most mornings – we had a coffee or two, a simple but leisurely breakfast and then gently departed to our morning activity. This laid-back approach changed on pack up day in which case it was all-systems-go by 8am.

Typically, we'd stay three to five nights in one location, and then allow a day for packing, driving, and re-erecting the camp. Most of our road trips were between 400 and 700km, which a month previously would have sounded like a long way. Now anything less than 500km qualified as an easy day. Once we made a 120 km round trip just to refill a gas bottle, and on another occasion we drove 300 km for lunch!

While talking about these long hauls, I think you should spare a moment's sympathy for Kath. I'll tell you why. Before leaving Brisbane I recorded my 750 all-time favourite songs onto CDs (yes, 750), which we played to keep us entertained during long-haul drives. These songs, being my favourites, meant that I knew *most* of the lyrics to *most* of the songs. And I love to sing along. Loudly. Unfortunately, I have a tragically ill-tuned singing voice. Alley cats caught under trailer wheels have made sweeter sounds that my version of *Cracklin' Rosie*. Poor Kath had to tolerate this cacophony for about four to eight hours on every driving day.

The only mitigating factor was that Kath is completely tone deaf, and therefore did not realise that my singing was so inordinately terrible. Ignorance was bliss.

After departing the Shark Bay/Denham region, we headed north along the coast to the town of Exmouth. The rain mercifully ceased. After stopping at the town caravan park for one night to recharge our batteries (literally — I mean the trailer and fridge batteries) we headed around the peninsular to Cape Range National Park, home to the wonderful Ningaloo reef.

The West Australian National Parks department has a frustrating system for allocating camping spots in their national parks. You cannot book a campsite. You cannot even buy a permit. You simply have to show up in the morning and hope to get a space on a first-come-first-served basis. Because the sites are very limited, you can only go in if someone else departs. If you miss out, you simply turn around and drive back, tail between your legs, from whence you came. You repeat the process the next day, again without any guarantees.

So it was with some trepidation — would we get in or not? - that we arrived about 7.45 am, bleary eyed, at the ranger's gate outside Cape Range National Park. Eight cars were ahead of us in the queue.

On tour so far, our luck when requesting accommodation had been incredibly good. Of the four caravan parks we had booked into so far, we were allotted the *last* available space on every occasion. Would our good fortune continue, or was it a tedious drive back to Exmouth and another try tomorrow?

I was mildly disappointed to learn that we had snuck into a spot, but it was only the *second last*, rather than the last, available site. I wanted to keep our roll going.

We were, of course, very happy to have made it through the hallowed gates of Cape Range, and had soon set up camp. It was a wonderful spot, just metres from a ledge that stepped down into the Indian Ocean. Naturally, the campsite had superb sunset views over the water. We couldn't wait to explore under the surface of that water, which was home to one of Australia's best coral reef systems. The kids and I were soon in our wet suits. Strange - mine seemed to have shrunk since I had last worn it about a year previously. This contraction, I figured, may have been due to the heat on the roof racks where they were stored, although it seemed odd that Kath's and the kids' suits were not similarly affected.

After donning our wetsuits, we swam across a 50 metre sand bar, whereupon we encountered the wonderful variety of underwater life that Ningaloo Reef has to offer. One advantage of this reef is that it exists relatively close to the mainland, as opposed to, say, the world famous Great Barrier Reef, which exists primarily on outlying islands and coral cays. So experiencing the coral, without a boat or a $350 day cruise ticket is very easy at Ningaloo.

To be brutally honest, the coral fell way short of the dazzling displays in the Great Barrier Reef in terms of quality, colour and abundance. On the positive side, the animal life was incredible. In just half an hour, we saw hundreds of fish, most of them brightly coloured, sprightly reef fish, dazzling in iridescent blue, Nemo-style stripes or any other rainbow-like combination you can imagine. There were also large schools of trevally, spiky sea urchins hiding in holes, and one very large, grumpy looking groper.

I entertained myself by throwing sea cucumbers at the kids, and by pretending to jam their fingers into the menacing-looking crevices of a giant clams. Bullying can be so much fun.

Yet for all the beauty and colour of the marine underworld, I simply could not resist sizing up anything that swam by for a spot on my dinner plate, beside some hand cut chips and a wedge of lemon. So that afternoon we hiked a kilometre out to the northern point of the bay. The guy in the tent next door had heard from the previous bloke that the fella in the tent down the row knew someone who had caught some fish there. We were going to have a nice relaxing afternoon of family fishing, and bring home supper to boot.

Half an hour later, I had not yet cast a line. I had simply oscillated between Lachie and Jake, untangling their lines in turn. They really tried hard to master the intricacies of the fisherman's bend knots, Alvey vs. spinner reel casting, and bait presentation, but sometimes fishing lines and six/eight-year-olds just do not mix.

Eventually Jake gave up and went back up the beach to play with (read: interrupt) Kath and Caitlin, who were busy doing not much at all. Lachie eventually sorted out his tangles and managed to keep his hook in the water for long enough for me to clip on a lure, and finally I was able to get into it.

Three hours later, I was still casting. The sun had set, the family had long since returned to camp, and the tide had risen to waist-deep. I had tried half a dozen combinations of sinker, hook, leader and lure, but without so much as a nibble. I even resorted to a few casts with the lucky lure that my mate Tod had given me as a going away present, but remained *sans* fish.

It would be easy to think that I went home frustrated and bored, but nothing could be further from the truth. There is something very therapeutic about flicking a lure over still water as the western sun sets over the ocean. But I admit a catch would have been nice.

*

The next morning again dawned bright and clear. Kath and the kids were keen for a walk along the foreshore, followed by a swim, but I had a better idea. After all, it was perfect fishing weather. Undeterred by my failure of the previous day (and my other failures on every day before that) I wandered down to the rocky foreshore directly in front of our camp. I had seen some big schools of fish there while snorkelling, so it made sense to target that area. Plus it meant I would only have to walk 20 metres back to camp with my anticipated huge haul, not a kilometre like yesterday.

It is with some pride that I must report that (drum roll please) – I caught a fish! (Rousing trumpet fanfare, cue the confetti.) And a bloody good one too. It was a speckled emperor, was about a metre long, and weighed 20 kg.

I wish. Ok, it wasn't a metre, and it didn't weigh 20 kg - more like 50 cm and 3 kg*. But it *was* a speckled emperor and it *was* big enough to supply four decent fillets for dinner.

Later that afternoon I also caught a reef cod while snorkelling with a hand line. The technique sounds simple: don your goggles and flippers, grab a baited hand line, swim around until you see a fish you like, and

---

* Ok, Ok. 35 cm and 1.5 kg.

then dangle the bait directly in front of its nose. Selective fishing. After it's ensnared itself you simply swim back to shore with your bounty.

In reality, it is not quite as simple. Big ugly humans like me tend to scare away delicate, skittish fish. And the swim back to shore with your hooked fish is a crazy, adrenalin-filled tug-o-war. Yet I managed to catch four fish using this unorthodox technique. Three of them were too small and far too pretty to eat, but one young spotted rock cod became fillets five and six.

Most of our week at Ningaloo Reef proceeded as such: an hour or so of snorkelling with the kids in the morning, throwing a line in somewhere, and the rest was just hanging around. However, we did manage to sneak away for two adventures: a whale shark dive, and a kayak tour.

Lachie accompanied me on the whale shark dive on the basis that he was the only family member who assured me that he wouldn't poop his pants at the thought of swimming beside a *seven metre long* shark.

Whale sharks are fish, not whales. They are so gargantuan that they are oblivious to predators, and are therefore unfazed by human company. Furthermore, they swim slowly enough that you can keep pace with them (just). Exmouth is the only place on Earth where they reliably come close to shore at regular times of the year, which presented us with a wonderful chance to experience a unique interaction with nature. And with that, of course, is the chance for a local boat operator to make $350 per head running the tour.

And so it was, heavy with anticipation but light on cash, that Lachie and I boarded a tourist ship called the *S.S.*

*Minnow** and headed into the open seas. Our first stop was at a coral cay for a snorkelling session to make sure everyone was familiar with his or her gear. The break also allowed time for the spotter plane to locate some whale sharks.

It was a very worthwhile stopover. The coral was fantastic, and the deeper water – this was six or seven metres – added a third dimension to the exploration. The highlight was a couple of manta rays that were gracefully doing laps of a coral bommie, along with the usual plethora of angel fish, parrot fish, colourful reef formations and amenomies ... anenami ... amena ... oh bugger it, soft corals.

After about an hour, the word came through the crackling radio: the spotter had sighted a whale shark. We sped off to the designated GPS point, with our boatload of punters growing more nervous by the minute. Quickly, our moment arrived. We sat on the back of the boat, and then plunged into the water, directly in the path of a behemothic whale shark.

The WA government has developed regulations that state that a swimmer may not approach within three metres of a whale shark. For me, this particular regulation was entirely unnecessary. I was so scared shitless that I wasn't going within ten metres of that baby. Lachie was even more chicken: he swam directly behind me, more or less blocking his own view of the monster.

---

* It wasn't really – that was the name of the ship on *Gilligan's Island*. (Google it if you're under the age of 35) I can't remember the real name

After a minute that was primarily spent noting that the whale shark hadn't eaten anyone yet, I cautiously swam closer. As we swam our way up towards the beast's head, I pulled Lachie by the hand in front of me to afford him a less obstructed view. He spent the rest of the day telling anyone who would listen that "daddy tried to push me into the whale shark's mouth".

I solemnly declare here, in writing, before you as my witness, that this thought did not even cross my mind. Not for long, anyway.

An underwater photograph of this moment snapped by the tour operator captured it perfectly; despite Lachie's features being completely concealed by diving goggles and a snorkel, you could actually see the terror in his face.

We were lucky enough to have four swims with the sharks. The first was brief – only a couple of minutes – but as the day went on they became longer. The last swim was, I guess, about seven or eight minutes. With each session, my fear faded, and eventually I was able to glide next to these big guys and appreciate their effortless movement, sheer bulk, and, in particular, their neat dental work. It was an experience to remember.

Perhaps a few of the oldies on the boat didn't fully agree with me. Like most places we visited in these remote areas, the clientele were primarily grey nomads. Of the 40 or so guests on the SS Minnow on this fateful trip, about 34 were of the retired variety.

I'm no Michael Phelps – in fact, I was one of the worst swimmers in my class at school - but these days I can swim a kilometre or so if necessary. But when swimming alongside the whale sharks, it took my fullest effort, kicking my fins ferociously, to keep up. The grey nomads behind me didn't stand a chance. After each swim finished, I'd look up, and there'd be a 500m long trail of heads, bobbing like grey buoys, back toward the boat. Most of them never got with cooee of the shark. They certainly didn't get much out of the experience apart from getting wet. "The ability to swim quickly for 5-8 minutes" was scandalously never mentioned as a pre-requisite on the brochures.

Our fun that day did not end with the whale sharks. On the final dive, only a handful of swimmers entered the water. The rest were either too buggered, or had long-since conceded any hope of keeping up. Lachie had also called it quits – unfortunately he had pooped his pants at the thought of swimming beside a seven metre long shark. Just kidding – he was just too buggered, and was starting to turn a mild shade of 'seasick green'.

After a couple of minutes with the whale shark, all the other swimmers except for the guide and I had fallen by the wayside. Effectively we had the beast to ourselves. Enter, stage right, a Minke Whale.

Imagine a gigantic, overgrown dolphin, and you'll have a fair picture of a Minke. It dived below us, appearing to check us out. The guide was beside himself with delight – he was understandably bored with the familiar whale sharks, but, as I learned later, the Minke was a new experience. However, the Minke show didn't end there. It swam in a large circle, and returned for another play a minute later. It repeated this performance four times in total. Nobody could explain why it did this. Perhaps it was a female Minke and was attracted by the sight of a male with a BMI of over 30 in a tight-fitting wetsuit.

Whatever the reason, I had the rare experience of swimming between a whale and a whale shark. It was quite a day.

Our next adventure was when Caitlin and I signed up for a guided kayak expedition. We were greeted at the boat ramp by a solid thirty-ish year old girl named Sandy, who was our group leader for the day.

At this point, I wish to pose a question: What is the stupidest thing you have ever thought about doing? Go on, think about it. I'm sure you've had at least one real howler. But more importantly, did you follow through this stupid thought and actually act on it? I hope not, although if you're anything like most of my mates, I have grave doubts.

I have included this preamble to add gravitas to my description of our venerable guide, Sandy. She had woken up in a perfectly good bed in Perth about a year before and thought: *Gee willikers*, wouldn't it be just a splendid and dandy thing to paddle to Darwin in a kayak.

Yes, I said Darwin. Yes, she was in Perth.

Just in case you're unawares, Darwin is about 6000km from Perth. In between are waters with massive tides, blistering sun, and ferocious, unforgiving animals such as salt water crocodiles. Up that way nature has a habit of throwing its nastiest weather at you, with a half a dozen wild tropical cyclones each year considered normal. Not to mention having to carry all of your bedding, shelter, furniture, food, televisions and beer with you on one small kayak.

Just to have that thought is ridiculous enough in itself, but to follow through with action is just ludicrous. But once it entered her head, young Sandy was hooked by her own nightmare – er, sorry - dream. She resigned from her teaching job, grabbed her kayak and set out up the coast. Woo-hoo, what a fun time - paddling for ten hours a day, eating nothing but dried apricots and beef jerky *for a year*.

Once she made it to Darwin, Sandy had a huge celebration, and did nothing but laze around, eating chocolate and pizza, drinking sunset cocktails, and sleeping in until noon every day. Well, that's what I would have done to make up for 12 months of self deprivation. She didn't. Sandy, who is clearly far more determined (and/or stupid) than I, simply turned her trusty kayak around and set out on her way back to Perth. She had since pulled up stumps in Exmouth for a while to help run the kayak tours.

By the way, she had very big deltoids.

After packing and setting up our boats, we casually paddled out into the blue yonder, with Caity up front in the bow, and me in the stern. I found the pace relaxing, but Caitlin kept complaining that her arms were tired and sore. I really don't know why. That girl has to toughen up a bit*.

The adventure unfolded as you would imagine. The day was sunny and cool, and the water was as clear and

---

* Please don't tell Caity, but I sat in the back for a reason: so that I could have frequent rests from paddling without her noticing. For much of the journey I did nothing at all except bark encouragement at her whilst semi-reclining in the back seat. Ah kids - you gotta love 'em.

calm as a millpond. Or lake. We paddled for a couple of hours, and then stopped for lunch and a session of snorkelling. Apart from the usual menagerie of fish we also saw half a dozen turtles, some angler fish with their strange "fishing lines" trailing behind them and a flute-nosed fish that, unsurprisingly, looked exactly like a flute would if it could swim.

Then we had a similarly relaxed paddle back to the boat ramp, although inevitably the horses bolted when they sniffed the home paddock. Caitlin and I won the "race" back to base, although I admit it was not via the usual channels of superior strength or stamina. We simply nabbed the inside lane and rammed anyone who tried to pass us.

The day ended with ex-schoolteacher Sandy ensuring that we had all washed, scrubbed, disinfected, cleaned, polished, dried and stacked away our kayaks before we were allowed to go home to play. Sort of like asking friends around for dinner and then insisting that they polish the silverware and run the Hoover around the dining room before departing. That aside, it was a worthwhile adventure.

*

The next day the wind picked up, and although we were getting nicely into the groove of seaside living, and getting quite used to the sunset drinks overlooking the ocean, we decided to head east to Karajini National Park. We packed up, drove back around the peninsular, through the town of Exmouth, then turned perpendicularly across the Great Northern Highway and headed inland. Then something very trivial happened that pleased me quite a lot.

Since the first day on the road, the kids had been pestering me with one question: "Dad, are we in the outback yet?" I patiently explained to them that the outback was a hazy, ill-defined notion, not a clear-cut issue, and that it would therefore be difficult to annunciate the precise moment that we hit "the outback".

However, they persisted with the question, which by now I was answering rather more succinctly with "No". However as we motored out of Exmouth that morning, the question was piped up again. This time, I was able to answer in the affirmative.

"Yes, kids, we are now officially in the outback."

How was I so sure? It was not the heat or the dust – they hadn't changed appreciably. Nor had the sparse, desert-like vegetation altered; it had been sparse and desert-like since suburban Perth. And nor was it that we were now leaving the coast. The factor that indicated that without doubt we were now in the outback was this: The Outback Motorists' Gidday Wave.

For the uninitiated city slickers among you, the Outback Motorists Gidday Wave works like this. First, you must appreciate that in this part of the world, you encounter a vehicle heading in the opposite direction perhaps only once every 15 minutes or so, even on the busiest roads. As you approach the car, your right hand briefly leaves the steering wheel and you offer a short but friendly gidday-type wave to the other driver. If he is a highly-skilled outback driver, the return wave will be simultaneous. Of course, you will never see this person again, and wouldn't recognise him if you reunited 10 seconds later, but the OMGW is given freely nonetheless.

My preferred embodiment is to simply protrude the index finger of my right hand off the steering wheel, combined with a slight nod of my head. Much more casual and refined than the frantic gesticulating of those Crazy Germans in their campervans, but at least they're *trying* to be friendly.

And so, in what seemed a miracle of collective intelligence, every car we passed on the road to Karijini gave us the OMGW. There were no signs to indicate that this was an appropriate road on which to perform this ritual. No committee had ever designated this as an OMGW road, nor was there a written code of practice. Everybody just intuitively knew to wave. It felt right.

Yes kiddies, we're now in the outback.

Chapter Six: Karijini

We soon received further confirmation that we were in the outback by way of another clear indicator: the prices for basic food and fuel. Down in the big smoke of Perth, petrol was hovering at around the $1.20 per litre mark. On tour to this point, its cost had been rising at about 5 cents per hour – i.e. roughly 5 cents for every 100km north. However, at Nannaturra Roadhouse, about 280 km inland from Exmouth, the price took a kangaroo-sized hop up to $2.05 per litre of standard unleaded fuel.

A standard price for a burger in the city was about $6.00 or $7.00. Nannaturra was also the home of the $17.00 hamburger - and that was the takeaway price! It cost an extra $5.00 if you wanted to sit on the nice plastic chairs inside instead of the old plastic chairs outside. Nannaturra's version of dining in.

While I think of it, there's another small thing that took me a while to get used to in Western Australia. At home on the east coast in Brisbane, if you want to come across as a country dude, you talk about "heading west". *Out West* is where the bush is, and where the men are tough and thirsty. *Out West* is where the land is large, the days are hot and the sheep are scared. Over here, that same veneer of rugged colonialism is achieved by talking about "heading east". It just didn't sound right.

After choking back five $17.00 burgers – no, not just me, I mean one for each member of the family - we headed east, to the mining town of Tom Price. This outpost was named after the original CEO of the mine, who was so instrumental in establishing the site that they named the whole town after him.

I am sure that the residents are forever grateful that the CEO wasn't a Russian or a Sri Lankan. Who would want to live in a town called Bogatyr Bagration-Mukhranskii or Kapila Wijegunawardene?

The mine was only supposed to last 15 years, but it has been going over 30 already. Due to high Chinese demand, and therefore the steeply rising price, of iron ore, it was now likely to go on for at least another 20 years - unlike poor old Tom, who kicked the bucket before a pick was struck in anger.

Originally we had travelled to Tom Price just for a quick overnight stay to stock up, charge up, and have a shower – it had been a while since we had done any of the three. We ended up staying an extra day to take on a mine tour. The excursion wasn't bad, with the key theme being that everything is BIG. Really big. For example, the tyres on the standard delivery trucks are 3.8 metres high.

That night, after setting up camp, we headed into the town centre. It was, well, compact. The CBD would comfortably fit inside an Olympic-sized swimming pool. After a couple of enquiries as to the best place for dinner, it emerged that the only place for a decent feed was at the pub. I put my hand up to investigate.

Not convivial, was my first thought. The beer-garden-cum-bar was a reasonable setting, but it appeared that the northern chapter of the combined Biker Gangs of Western Australia was having its AGM that night. In truth, it was probably just a bunch of thirsty miners letting off some steam after a hot and hard day's work, but it wasn't the ideal setting for a quiet family dinner.

So imagine my delight when one small, unmarked door in the corner of the bar opened into a huge, well-appointed dining room, with nice little waitresses prancing around smoothing down the white-linen tablecloths. I was already sold but when I spotted the magic words *All you can eat buffet* on a sign above the kitchen I couldn't get the troops in there quickly enough.

My happiness was further magnified after I had delivered the beer, chardonnay, and three glasses of pink lemonade to the table. I heard a familiar tune – the Aussie national anthem – coming from a television set in the corner. I investigated, and discovered that we had stumbled across an Australia vs. South Africa rugby test match, one of the sporting highlights of the year. At home, I would have been devouring every aspect of this match for a week before kickoff, but on tour in outback WA, I hadn't even realised that the test series was underway. Then again, I hadn't even realised that it was Saturday.

The random discovery of an international Rugby match illustrates a factor of our itinerant lifestyle: we were effectively quarantined from the outside world. We heard no news, read no papers, generally used no internet or telephone, and watched no television. At home, I did all of these every day without fail. Out here, a war could start and we wouldn't know it until we saw the mushroom cloud. Which, let's face it, is a nice way to be. The isolation is nice – not the nuclear explosion.

The buffet was fine. The Cheapskate Traveller's Code of Conduct was called into practice after dinner, when we borrowed a few of those little tomato sauce and mayonnaise containers; you know, the ones that you squeeze together to break the seal, and then you squirt the sauce on your chips, and then discard the packet with about three quarters of the sauce still inside. Well, I suppose we didn't really borrow them; that would imply that we intended to return them. Yet it would be harsh to say that we stole, purloined, or pilfered them; after all, we had paid for the dinner, which included the little sauce packets. Perhaps we should settle on the word "liberated". Either way, the cheapskates' code allowed for the liberating of a few little sauce packets to re-stock our camp supplies. By the way, the same rule holds true for the little salt and pepper packets at McDonalds, drinking straws at road-stop garages, and tissue-paper napkins wherever you find them.

No kiddies, the rule does not also hold true for televisions in department stores.

*

The next morning we departed Tom Price for the gorge capital of the Pilbara region, Karijini National Park. After setting up camp, I headed off to the communal barbeque to cook up our evening feed. There was a grey nomad of the female persuasion occupying half of the plate – well, her food was anyway. She offered me the spare half to cook on. At first she seemed like a friendly, chatty old duck ...it didn't take me long to change that opinion.

After quickly dispensing with pleasantries, she informed me that the nights were very cold at Karijini. In fact, the temperature had dropped to minus 0.4 degrees that very morning. She knew that it had reached exactly minus 0.4 degrees because she had three thermometers and had averaged them out.

She also instructed me that I wasn't seasoning my camp oven properly, that I should avoid back packers (and young people in general) as they were all credit card thieves, and that we should tie down our annex more tightly so that it didn't flap in the wind. Furthermore, the torch I was carrying wouldn't be good enough to see the roof of a nearby attraction called Tunnel Creek. It was *insufficient*, to use her word. She then stepped over the line by commenting unfavourably on my steak-cooking technique. I nearly clipped her with my insufficient torch.

The next day dawned cold and clear – by my guess it was just a touch below zero, probably about -0.4^0 Celsius. But as the sun rose the temperature escalated by about a degree every ten minutes, leading to a fine, warm day. Nature could not have been kinder to us as we set out to explore the gorges.

Karijini is where old photographers go when they die. In every direction tower red-rocked cliffs, tumbling waterfalls or cool blue pools. There's a postcard view at every turn. The whole area boasts natural riches like Hollywood boasts silicone.

Exploring these gorges was like walking through a gigantic kids' playground obstacle course. The tracks ranged from simply walking along dry sandy riverbeds, to rock climbing, to wading through water. There were a couple of ladder descents, and even some basic abseiling down set ropes. It was a blast. Kath, you will be relieved to hear, survived this ordeal with nary a scratch. In fact, I think she begrudgingly enjoyed it.

To spare you further glowing descriptions of Karajani's rugged beauty, and to free up some time so that I can nab a glass of wine before bed, might I suggest that you Google the nearest computer for some pictures of this remote wonderland. Despite my most earnest efforts as a wordsmith, I simply cannot do it justice. Better still, book a holiday there.

We'd experienced all sorts of wildlife on our trip to this point: from the multitude of marine creatures that we'd interacted with, to kangaroos and wallabies to emus and quokkas. Also that feral cat I tried to run over. At Karijini, Kath and I had a wildlife encounter that we'd rather forget.

Just after we arrived, the campers next door warned us that a dingo had ransacked their food supplies the night before, so we were wary from the start. Our incident occurred late on the second night. The sky was deeply black – the kind of dark in which you can't see the tree in front of your face until you've walked into it. Kath had left the tent for a midnight toilet stop, which had roused me from my sleep. In the distance, I heard the unmistakable howl of a dingo. Being the macho husband that I am, I turned over and tried to go back to sleep. Hey, it was freezing out there.

However, a minute later I decided that I, too, had to relieve myself, so I stumbled out of the tent, groggy with sleep, and groping in the dark. I was relieving myself by the side of the tent – it's a big advantage being male in that part of the world - when Kath returned from the ablutions block. Just as we exchanged groggy, late night hellos, we heard a low, long, deep growl.

The sound emanated not more than a few metres from where we both stood, now frozen to the spot. Kath clutched my arm as we stood in the cold darkness, trying to discern an outline. A few seconds later, there was another long, low, rumbling growl.

"Quick, give me your torch," I whispered to Kath. As I said this, I was hoping that she had picked out my big long metal torch – it's so solid it's more like a weapon than a torch – and not the insufficient little plastic one that had already been the source of derision from our condescending neighbour. Thankfully, Kath handed over the truncheon-torch. But before I had time to switch it on, we heard a third low grumbling growl, but this time with more deep-throated menace.

This, I surmised, was bad news. Dogs, in my experience, barely give you one warning growl before they attack. This predator had already given us three warnings, and was ready to pounce. And maim. Maybe kill.

With all the courage I could muster, I flicked on the beam.

Nothing.

Then I heard the fourth growl. I shone the torch beam frantically back and forth, trying to spot the beast that sounded like it was now way too close. Then, inexplicably, Kath started to laugh.

Now I'm all for trying to stay calm in a crisis, but *laughing?* We were in the deep Australian outback, hours from medical help, on the darkest of nights, with a dangerous-sounding dog growling only metres away. I was having thoughts of Azaria Chamberlain, which, to those who don't know that tragic story, was far from funny. How could Kath be *laughing*?

Then I got it too. It wasn't a dingo we were hearing. It was the dulcet tones of one eight-year-old Jacob Perrier, just inside the tent, peacefully snoring.

Back inside the safe confines of our canvas castle, we rolled Jake onto his side to stop the noise. Even so, it took an hour before my heart rate dropped below 150. Didn't get much sleep that night.

This incident, despite its benign ending, illustrates that Australia is home to a bewildering array of deadly animals. If the crocodiles and sharks don't eat you, then a stonefish, box jellyfish, king brown snake or scorpion will make you wish they had. But none of these things worried me before we set off for the trip.

All sorts of things can (and were about to) go wrong on a trip like this: mechanical breakdowns, illness, or injury, just to name a few. I had packed as many spares and tools as possible, along with a comprehensive first aid kit, so I wasn't worried about those types of problems either. But there were two situations that I just couldn't solve in advance, no matter how hard I focused.

The first was - and I am phrasing this delicately, primarily for the benefit of any near-relatives who are reading: How was I going to, well, you know, be, er, intimate, in the campervan? A campervan is not the most private of confines in which a couple can spend three minutes expressing their everlasting love for each other, is it?

The problem with such activities was spelled out to me by a good friend who had previously been on a similar campervan holiday in Western Australia. Because this story is embarrassing for him, I won't use his real name. Instead, I'll call him *Terry*. Before leaving on his trip, Terry had rigged up a neat system for storing all the kitchen pots, pans and large utensils. He created a rack from which they all hung that he suspended in their campervan annexe. For the first few days of the trip, this system worked well.

Eventually the time came when Terry wished to do the married couple thing with his wife, who, for purposes of discretion, I will call Sally. Just as young Terry was getting into his rhythm, they heard a cacophony from outside the tent. Terry and Sally's exertions had transformed the suspended kitchen utensils into a clanking, clanging, wind-chime-on-steroids, gaily advertising to all and sundry that there was movement at the station. The jingle-jangle of the pots was informing all that some jingly-jangly was happening inside.

It was against this backdrop, along with the knowledge that we had three children sharing the tent, that I embarked upon our journey. I must admit that I could not think of a single reliable solution.

I won't go into detail, but you'll be pleased to know that I solved this problem. You can read about it in my next book, a fully illustrated tome entitled *Campervan Kama Sutra II: 101 ways to have sex in a campervan without the kids or neighbours knowing*.

OK, I admit it wasn't 101 ways. In fact, I only came up with thirty four.

Nevertheless, you can safely assume that my first unsolvable worry was mitigated. My second major worry was this: tyres. Flat ones, to be precise.

Before leaving on this trip, we had heard horror stories about some of the northern roads. We'd heard tales of sharp road stones ripping tyres to shreds, and of people being stranded for days with a flat. I had taken every sensible precaution to avoid these sorts of dramas – I'd purchased three new tyres, a tyre repair kit, and carried two good spares. But if a sharp rock deliberately aims itself for the centre of your tread, there's not much you can do about it. In the northern section of Karijini National Park, the truth of this pre-trip worry hit us.

We were travelling to the north of the park, just past a town called Wittenoom. Wittenoom is now a ghost town after they made the unfortunate discovery that many of the residents were dying of cancer caused by the town's asbestos mine. (We took *very shallow breaths* as we drove past.) The road was very remote, with virtually no traffic whatsoever. We hadn't passed another car for an hour or so when a couple – it turned out that they were siblings named Daryl and Tracey- flagged us down by the roadside.

The previous evening, at about 6 pm, they had suffered a flat tyre. They changed to their spare, and headed off again. Five minutes later another tyre had been shredded and they had been stranded since. Apart from a solitary vehicle that had passed by at 8 pm the previous evening, we were the only people they had seen since.

I looked at my watch. It was noon. These people has already been waiting nearly 20 hours in the middle of nowhere for help.

We did our best to assist them, but both of their tyres were cactus. We agreed to drive on ahead and ring the local automobile rescue club, as well as notifying Tracey's husband. Midway through the conversation Daryl glanced down at the rear right tyre of our Jackeroo.

"Looks like you might need a bit of air in that tyre before you go," he offered. I checked it myself, and was surprised to notice that it did, indeed, look a bit flat.

Unfortunately, the tyre continued slowly deflating as we watched, and soon it was evident that it was, in fact, stuffed. We enjoyed the irony as *Daryl* helped *me* change *our* flat tyre. We soon drove off with promises to send help, leaving them only a cloud of dust and the same roadside view they had enjoyed for 20 hours thus far.

Just five minutes later, I heard an almighty bang from the same rear right tyre of the Jackeroo. This time there was no doubt: the tyre had a massive hole. Unlike Daryl and Tracey, we had a second spare, and so another half an hour of sweaty work ensued. I was already covered in red dust from head to toe from the first tyre change, but by the time I had replaced the second I was positively filthy, even by camping standards. Even the old trick of wearing my clothes inside out for the first two days couldn't save these particular garments from an early dispatch to the dirty clothes bag.

It was not a nice feeling: being in the middle of nowhere, without another spare tyre, driving on a road that we knew had claimed four tyres in as many kilometres. The roadside rocks were razor sharp, and shaped like arrowheads. One more puncture and we would be stuck in the dust like Daryl and Tracey for who knows how long?

Rather than continuing our journey northward, we reversed our direction and, very gingerly, at 40 km/h, drove back the way we had come in. I don't know if driving slowly makes you less likely to get a puncture, but it seemed like a good idea at the time. We knew that there was a bitumen road only 80 km back – as opposed to 300 km of razor sharp rocks if we continued.

I can only guess at Daryl and Tracey's emotions as we rounded the bend and came back into their view. Probably initial excitement – was help finally arriving? - then familiarity, mixed with confusion, followed by frustration. We stopped for another chat about our common experience, and left with further promises to send help.

Two nail-bitingly-anxious hours later, we finally hit the tar near Wittenoom. We all breathed a heavy sigh of relief, no doubt raising our risk of mesothelioma in the process.

Wittenoom was a strange, and, in many ways, sad, town. It could not have been any more ghost-like had it put a white sheet over its head and floated through the air. Wittenoom was once a solid little metropolis of about 500 people living in 150 or so dwellings. Then, in the 1970s, after the health dangers associated with asbestos became apparent, the nearby mine closed down, thereby suffocating the town's only true employment source.

People departed in droves. For the next couple of decades the government produced, as governments often do, plenty of talk, and many glossy reports, discussing the town's rehabilitation. The prime difficulty lay in clearing away the asbestos-laden topsoil; about a foot of dirt had to be scraped away from the entire township. In the end, one of the shiny reports deemed that the rejuvenation was too expensive and difficult, sealing Wittenoom's fate. The final indignity came in 2007 when the WA government officially degazetted the town; they removed it from all maps, and never again referenced it in any government material. In short, it ceased to exist.

These days, a drive around the streets of Wittenoom is to see not the skeleton of a town, but a fossil. Nearly all of the buildings have been demolished, leaving only the old roads and gutters as a life-sized map of what the town used to look like. There are no government services such as electricity, police, or health, and it is searingly hot and humid all year round. The surrounding countryside is so barren, rocky and desolate that if Hollywood ever needs a ready-made set for a first-person-on-Mars movie, Wittenoom has it ready and waiting. Very few cars pass this way, so there is scant tourism. If that all wasn't bad enough, government signs warn visitors not to stop at Wittenoom lest they breathe in a stray particle of asbestos that was still peskily floating through the air 40 years after the mine closed. Grade one arse covering, methinks.

Yet despite all these clear disadvantages and deterrents, about a dozen extremely hardy souls still call Wittenoom home. Their houses sit huddled together in one corner of the town, reminding me of the last sandcastles on a beach, still standing as the rising tide razes all else flat. What they do for kicks around here I can barely imagine. Even Tom Price, the nearest town, is more than 100 km of tyre-stripping dirt road away; that's a fair ride in a cab after going to the pub on Saturday night.

I wanted to wander around the little enclave of houses, hopefully to meet up with a local or two, just to find out what makes them tick. You would really have to love peace and quiet, not to mention dust, heat, and isolation, to permanently pitch your tent here. You'd also want a sizeable portion of your fortune put aside for new tyres.

However, Kath demurred, at first gently, and then with insistence. The government warning signs had done the trick; she thought it was too dangerous to even wind down the car window, much less depart the sanctity of our vehicle. I tried to explain to her, using my patient, logical voice, that the chances of a stray asbestos particle still bobbing about on the breeze after four decades was virtually nil, and that even if we inhaled a lungful of them the odds of contracting cancer were similarly negligible. I illustrated this point with the salient fact that although thousands of people worked on this mine every year, merrily drilling, cutting and breathing asbestos all day long for decades on end, only an unfortunate handful of them contracted lung cancer.

My entreaties fell upon deaf ears. For some reason this always happens when I use my patient logical voice. Kath could not be convinced, so the windows stayed firmly up, the car stayed in gear, and we soon departed Wittenoom without having bothered the locals.

In time we made it to Auski Roadhouse, not far from where we had started the day's journey. We made a call on behalf of our stranded duo, and then located the tyre repair guy. Apparently, our tyres were unrepairable, so we decided to stay for the night and head up the paved road to the larger town of Port Hedland the next morning.

Normally a one-night camp at a roadhouse in the middle of a boring stretch of featureless highway would not rate a mention in a grandiose tome such as this. But it had been a hot and anxious day, and it was just nice to be *somewhere*. I enjoyed one of the most anticipated hot showers I have ever experienced, and celebrated further by putting on my clothes the right way, rather than inside-out, on the first day.

The family then repaired to the local restaurant – the roadhouse - for dinner. I ordered the mixed grill, and grabbed a couple of stubbies of beer to help wash it down. I could barely believe my eyes when the meal arrived. They must have slaughtered a cow, a couple of pigs, a roo or two, and probably a goanna, to get this much meat on one plate. It had three bits of steak (two fillets and a T-bone), a couple of sausages, a mound of bacon, two eggs on toast, assorted hunks of tomato and mushroom, and enough chips to start a poker tournament. I was just wondering how I was going to devour this behemoth in front of me when the waitress piped up:

"The mixed grill comes with complimentary salad – the all-you-can-eat salad bar is in the corner. Help yourself."

I know a challenge when I hear one. The buffet had six different salads. I heaped on a large spoonful of each until the food mound on my plate was fully half a foot high.

I polished off every morsel. Didn't even give the kids a chip.

That night, I went to bed feeling unusually happy and content. Despite a very trying day, I can rarely recall feeling as satisfied. The smile was somewhat wiped off my face after two hours of reflux that night (why does every indulgence have a price these days?) and further reversed in Port Hedland the next morning where two new tyres set me back $580. But such is the cost of travelling a smidgen outside your comfort zone. And so ended our exploration of Karijini, and, with that, the entire Pilbara area.

Oh wait, I almost forgot ...the highlight of the trip to Karijini – nay, of the entire trip so far – was my discovery near our next camp site of two stout trees about five metres apart. It was the first time since Perth that I had seen a pair of trees as such. I'm sure you can guess why I was so excited by this discovery. No?...

Chapter Seven: Pardoo Station

The trees? Let's just say I did my best to make the next part of our trip sound action packed, but it's difficult to distil too many thrills from a fortnight that consisted primarily of lying in a hammock. But don't worry, because wherever there was a boring patch I simply invented some good stuff.

We departed the inland sanctuary of Karijini National Park and headed back to the WA coast, ending up at a coastal bush camp called Pardoo Station. We had not intended to stop there; Pardoo barely rated a mention on our collection of maps and guidebooks. We had noticed it simply because we had driven past a sign, pointing off the highway toward the coast that read "Bush camp – cold beer – fishing." Five magic words. I couldn't turn the car around quickly enough. I'm glad we made the detour.

Pardoo is a working cattle station; its bona fides were immediately evident through the loud, agonised mooing and incessant braying associated with their four-day-long annual cattle muster. The cacophony was annoying at first, especially at night. However, after a day or so we all got used to it and in time it leant the place an agreeable country feel.

I can't blame the young bulls for kicking up a stink. I'd probably make a similar sound if I were offered the same two options: decapitation or castration. Not much of a choice, really.

Like an increasing number of stations, Pardoo took in campers to supplement its farming income. It was instantly one of my favourite sites so far. It had a friendly, welcoming vibe, unlike some of the big caravan parks that are crammed full of grey nomads inside their 100ft caravans, doing crosswords, watching day time TV and checking their thermometers.

Pardoo also had a few luxuries. But before you become too excited on Kath's behalf about the sumptuous surrounds, let me define the term *luxury*. Two months previously my idea of luxury was, let's say, an hour's massage from a pretty little masseuse, followed by a few cold drinks of rare bourbon at a well-appointed bar. After that, I'd enjoy a meal of aged rib fillet accompanied by a bottle of Grange, before retiring with my beautiful wife to an upmarket hotel that had really good room service, movies on demand, and fresh linen.

Now my idea of luxury was a tap with the letter 'H' on it.

So the extravagances to which I am referring are bush-camp luxuries: a little shop that sold basic food items and cold beer, a cafe of sorts, 24-hour power, internet access, hot showers and flushing dunnies – all little touches that you don't get at national parks or free camps.

Pardoo Station campsite had lots of 'regulars'. Many of the old timers would stay for three months every year, and had been doing so since, oh, about the end of the Great War. Others had arrived intending to stay only a few nights, but were still hanging around a year later, unable to break the fiercely strong chains of Pardoo's de-motivating relaxation.

Best of all, Pardoo had a whopping communal fireplace. So far on tour, we had not encountered a single campsite that allowed fires –I have touched upon this issue previously. The lack of campfire-filled evenings had been one of the few disappointments of our trip. Pardoo quickly made up for this frustration.

Every evening at 5 pm, a station hand would dump a load of firewood at the circle, and one of the regulars would get the blaze going. As the evening progressed, the campers would steadily filter in, culminating in a peak of about 20 happy souls sipping beers and discussing the day's fishing catch. This cheerful little routine happened every night, and was a wonderful way to swap a yarn.

The kids *finally* got to toast their marshmallows. These particular marshmallows had travelled all the way from Brisbane for this moment – altogether about 10 000 km. If they had emotions, these marshmallows would no doubt be mightily satisfied to finally be devoured after such an arduous journey.

On our first afternoon at Pardoo, we took an exploratory drive along the coastline. After half an hour, we arrived at the creek that formed the northernmost boundary of the station. Its name was Barrabulomba or Waggagomba, or something vaguely aboriginal sounding that I simply could not commit to memory. Whatever its name, it had a lovely sandy foreshore leading down to a wide brown creek. If I were a fish, I would be happy to call this river home. I determined to return with my fishing weapons and try my luck.

If you have been paying attention thus far, then you would appreciate that my luck (read: ability) at fishing so far on this trip had been ordinary. On our second day at Pardoo, my fortunes changed. Armed with nothing more than an old coke can for a reel, a length of string, a bent paperclip for a hook and some stale bread as bait, I pulled in seven large bream in two hours.

OK, I really used my best fishing rod and some fresh squid, but the part about the bream was true. And they were all whoppers, which meant that they put up a decent rod-bending fight all the way to shore. For two hours it wasn't relaxing and tranquil, which are the words I usually use to describe a (failed) fishing trip. This session was an adrenalin-fuelled buzz.

The next day I returned with the kids and it happened all over again. I still had to perform the usual zigzagging between kids, untangling lines and re-baiting hooks, but at least we were pulling in dinner. Between us we snagged five beautiful salmon and two bream in an hour.

One aspect of fishing I appreciate is that while it is sometimes a fun-filled adrenaline rush, it also has serene, soothing moments. Nowhere exemplified this Jekyll-and-Hyde quality more than Pardoo. Over the next few afternoons, as the high tide roughly coincided with dusk, I sat calmly fishing on the riverbank as the stillness of the water increased with its growing depth. The sky, bereft of even the faintest of clouds, slowly turned from blue to pink, then to orange, lilac and finally navy. And then, amidst the serenity....jiggle, pause, jiggle jiggle, WHACK! You beauty, I'm on again! Feels like a salmon.

Sometimes another camper or two was present along the bank, but usually I was alone. Once I shared the riverbank with a local aboriginal woman, who was squatting on her haunches, hauling in salmon with nothing more than the aforementioned coke-can-and-piece-of-string rig, adorned with a simple sinker and a hook. She looked like part of the landscape. Her calm, almost spiritual presence made me feel like I was too.

Another activity at Pardoo was to watch the tide come in. I understand if you would normally rate this activity alongside button sorting, oven scrubbing, or watching non-world cup soccer matches. However, this activity was more interesting than it sounds due to the amazing tidal flows in this part of the world.

At Pardoo, the low tide to the high water mark covers an incredible *three kilometres*. To fully appreciate this movement, imagine this: You walk down to your local beach, set your towel down at the water's edge, rub on some coconut oil, plug in your walkman, and then drift into a little six-hour beach nap. If, upon awakening, you wanted to wash the sand out of your jandals, your return stroll to the water's edge would take you about an hour!

When the tide is flowing in at Pardoo, you can literally visualise it as an advancing wall of water about one centimetre high. My maths tells me that it moves about half a kilometre per hour, which, Kath assures me, is roughly eight or nine metres per minute. I've backed horses that have run slower than that.

Another thing that I learned at Pardoo is the importance of water conservation in the outback. I am sure that you are aware that these dusty dry stations have very limited water supply and that the farmers have to be extremely careful with every drop.

Sorry, but that last paragraph was complete crap. Pardoo, like most stations in this part of the world, has access to virtually unlimited supplies of clean bore water. We arrived on the first afternoon to see a flotilla of high pressure sprinklers soaking what was essentially dust. Most of the water either ran away, or created mud pools.

Before we had departed on our holiday, our home city of Brisbane had experienced a prolonged drought. Dams were holding only 10% capacity of water. The whole state was under Level Six water restrictions, which, as I recall, meant that each day all residents were limited to one shot-glass of drinking water, no showers or bathing of any sort, and that all cleaning of dishes and clothing must be done in an egg cup. Something like that anyway. So to see hundreds of litres of this precious fluid being squirted indiscriminately into the Pardoo dust was a bit provoking.

We came to realise that the whole top end is much the same: it has an abundance of clean water, with no hint of economy of usage. They literally have water to burn. This situation still strikes me as incongruous with the surrounding desert landscape.

One morning at Pardoo, a young aboriginal boy peered around our tent wall. He was very friendly, and chatted with us as though we were old mates. We learned that his name was Che; he asked if the boys could come and play. With the alternative being another hour or two of schoolwork, they couldn't get on their bikes quick enough.

We learned that Che had been living at Pardoo with his mother for about six months. They had been travelling down the coast en route to Perth when their car had broken down, and they hadn't yet saved enough for a replacement. They had simply pitched their tent at the station, and hadn't moved since.

This might sound like a wonderfully carefree way to live; as mentioned above, many people came to Pardoo for a brief getaway but ended up staying far longer. However, this lifestyle presented a small problem for young Che – interaction with children his own age. This part of the world was occupied almost exclusively by older travellers and outback workers: miners, jackaroos and the like. There were very few children. Young Che was thrilled to discover a rare tent-full of ready-made playmates.

He virtually moved in with us for the next few days; he fished with us, swam with us, ate with us, and played with the boys almost non-stop. The only time he disappeared was when the kids were doing schoolwork. Even then he popped back every five minutes to check if they were finished yet. Despite his ever-present-ness he was a nice kid, and a fine tour guide to the best fishing spots. He could even tie his own fishing knots.

Our lives ticked along at a very lazy pace at Pardoo. Kath and I spent our mornings chatting and drinking coffee, while Caity did schoolwork and the boys played with Che. I also spent plenty of time in my hammock, just reading or snoozing. In the afternoon, the kids swam in the station pool and rode their bikes, or went fishing with me. Kath managed to squeeze in a facial from a travelling beautician who had a placard outside her van. After dinner it was off to the fire for a few beers, to swap travel stories or boast about the day's catch. We repeated this languid routine each day.

On our fourth morning in Pardoo, I awoke with a mild hangover – not one of those seething, retching ones – just more a doughy headache and a dry mouth. After reading this far you should be aware that I enjoy a drink or two, so a mild hangover is not something that would normally rate a mention in my scribblings. But it was my first hint of a hangover so far on the trip. I guess the adult company around the campfire, including some Crazy German backpackers, had spurred me to exceed my unusually modest trip average of about three drinks per night.

I took this as a sign from above that we had stayed long enough, and we decided to depart the next day. But I made sure I really tied one on that night. Even outlasted the Crazy Germans.

Chapter Eight: Broome

After leaving the fisherman's paradise of Pardoo, we headed to the northern metropolis of Broome. Our first stop was the visitor's centre to grab some maps and brochures.

We were dirty and dishevelled. That WA dust has a way of making you filthy within five minutes of your shower. It's a shame the casting agents for the musical *Oliver* weren't around, because we could have shown up to the audition in character. In a bush camp setting this rustic appearance is fine, and no one expects any different. But now that we were in the big city, Kath suddenly became concerned about our appearances. She made everyone wipe their hands and face. She also insisted … wait for this … that we wear shoes.

After five long minutes of child preening I felt that the cleansing had gone far enough, and refused to further wipe my face, or don footwear, in protest. For heaven's sake, we were only popping into the tourist centre, not attending a Royal wedding. This was Broome, not Buckingham Palace. We were 5000km from home, in a distant outpost of Western Australia, so it's not as if we were going to bump into anyone we knew.

"Oh, hi! Look, it's the Perrier family," were the first words I heard as we passed though the visitor centre doors. We had bumped into Caitlin's grade one teacher, Mrs Irwin. As we made small talk, I surreptitiously manoeuvred myself behind a brochure stand to obscure the fact that I was shoeless.

I hate it when Kath is rrr...rrrii....riiight.

We duly trundled off to explore the townscape. My early opinion of Broome was: Hmmmm. Let me explain my lack of enthusiasm. If you are about my age (forty something), you can probably remember when your local beach was a wonderful, earthy, family place to vacation. I don't think I'm being over-nostalgic, or donning the rose-coloured-history glasses, when I make such assertions. You had fun in the sun and surf all morning until you were pink with sunburn, bought an ice cream on the way back for lunch, and then lay in the shade in the heat of the day. Toward dusk, you would go for a long family walk along the beach, or perhaps fly a kite as the afternoon breeze stiffened. For me, this place was the nearby Gold Coast.

As the tourists arrived en masse, out went the charm. The beach dunes were replaced by malls, the gardens bulldozed for shopping centres, and beachside parks were filled with skyscrapers. The Gold Coast has largely become a tawdry tourist-swallowing troll. Byron Bay, in northern New South Wales, has gone the same way: Sun and surf are secondary to T-shirt shops and   souvenirs.

Broome strikes me as a little beach town that's trying to become the Gold Coast when it grows up. If it's not careful, it will get what it's wishing for.

The Chinatown quarter of Broome is cited as being its centre of multiculturalism. This area is held up as an example of how Broome's historical Asian pearl-diving links produced a melting pot of inter-racial customs, foods and traditions. But apart from one Chinese restaurant selling $10 fried rice baskets for lunch, I could not see any evidence of ethnic influence. Instead, there were T-shirt shops, tour booking centres and souvenir outlets. Oh, and about 50 jewellery shops, all selling pearls. To my admittedly untrained eye there was no genuine Asian ethnicity whatsoever.

However, Broome (like the Gold Coast and Byron Bay) is not totally without its charms. Cable beach is a perfectly nice bay, with white-ish sand and blue water. It has some nice bars and cafes above it, from which we watched a frolicking pod of whales pass by. We splashed around in surf for an hour or so before heading off for the regulation Cable Beach Camel Ride. It's the postcard shot of any trip in the area.

The ride itself progressed much as you would imagine. Apart from when the camels stood up and down, which was a bit rocky, it was much like riding upon a walking horse. However, this tour came with a twist: the northern stretch of Cable Beach, upon which the camel treks take place, is a nudist beach.

I have a theory, which was strengthened at Cable Beach, that only two types of people sunbake naked in public. First, there are the wizening, leathery old men, who strut around with their dingy-jangly bits dangling and jingling, oblivious to the fact that they should feel embarrassed. The second typical group of nudists are gorgeous, voluptuous young females, hard at work eliminating the bikini lines on their tans.

Depending upon your predilection, if you can ignore one group and focus on the other, the experience can be reasonably gratifying. It took all of my concentration and mental energies, but I managed to achieve this cerebral feat whilst bobbing along upon a salivating camel. In particular, the vision of two unclad buxom young English women, who were genuinely surprised to see 26 jockeyed camels parading through their private little sand dune, made the $40 fee all the more reasonable.

Our other adventure in Broome was a ride with Jacob on a Harley-Davidson trike. It was, in essence, an individual guided tour of the Broome region, with the added benefit that, if you goaded the guide enough, he would chuck wheelies.

Jake joined me in the pillion seat for this little outing. He had a continuous smile on his face for the entire two hour experience. I'm not sure whether it was the thrill of speed, the joy of sitting on a Harley, or whether I had just put his goggles on too tightly.

The guide gave us some vouchers as part of the package. All you had to do was turn up to the local boutique brewery named Matso's, hand over the ticket, and they would give you, *free*, a long cold glass of the local produce. What a lovely concept. I duly cashed in my voucher. I used Jacob's as well – I traded him for a pink lemonade. Little did he know that beer cost $1.50 more than lemonade. Ha! There's a sucker born every minute.

Matso's also had an upmarket restaurant, at which we again bumped into Mrs Irwin. I think she was stalking us to check whether I was wearing shoes. Never have I been more pleased to have donned footwear for the evening, and I furtively demonstrated this fact to Mrs Irwin, lest she be on the verge of reporting to the primary school staff in Brisbane that John Perrier possessed no social graces whatsoever. Which, at the very least, would be an exaggeration.

We spent the rest of our time in Broome in the standard tourist traps, most of which were fine: the pearling museum, wandering around China town or the local markets, or heading down Gantheaume Point, south of cable beach, to see the fossilised dinosaur footprints. A quick warning if you wish to view the said dinosaur footprints for yourself. At our first visit, we wandered around the rocky headland for an hour without spotting anything resembling footprints. We asked a local woman for directions; she duly obliged, pointing us straight out to sea. "But you'll have to come back at low tide," she added. "They're covered by water when the tide's up."

We dutifully returned at low tide that afternoon, and again spent a fruitless half an hour wandering about the rocks, mistakenly attributing an ancient dinosaur's feet to anything that so much as resembled a pothole. Again, I had to take an ego hit, and ask for directions.

"Out that way," said the man, pointing directly into the ocean. "But you'll have to come back at low tide."

"But it *is* low tide," I gently protested.

"No, I mean the low-low tide," he replied. "This is the high-low tide."

Of course. Silly duffer me - we had come at the wrong low tide[3]. We duly returned a few days later, at the correct low tide, whereupon we stumbled upon some divots in the rocks that did, indeed, look like dinosaur footprints.

The other good thing about Broome was that it had a bike shop. You may recall from our earlier misadventures that somebody had backed the camper trailer into a post, completely buggering my bicycle in the process. So, when I spotted the bike shop, I could not resist a browse.

I quickly spotted a flash-looking, hi-tech bike with all the bells and whistles: it had precise gear mechanisms, great aerodynamics, an ultra light frame and wheels, and adjustable suspension. I walked straight past it, toward the cheap, basic models out the back. Half an hour later, I pedalled out of the shop on my brand new $260 mountain bike. Sure, it was bottom of the range, weighed a ton, and could best be described as 'clunky'. But it *was* shiny.

Having already destroyed one bike, I was determined to be more careful with this spanking new machine. I ensured that my bike was on the *bottom* of the rack, so that if some idiot put a post behind the trailer again, it would be the kids' crappy bikes that copped the dent, not my glossy new mount.

*

---

[3] For those readers who do not know what I am talking about, there are two low tides every day: one is the "high" low tide, while the other is the "low" low tide. In a place like Broome, which has very large tidal flows, this discrepancy can make a big difference to water depth.

Four days later, I returned to the same bike shop. I presented the attendant with a bike that had two bent tyre rims, a twisted crank shaft, two ruined tyres, and numerous snapped cables. It was filthy, grazed, scratched, and was so covered in dust and dirt that you couldn't even discern its original colour.

Yep, you guessed it –my new bike.

On the road out of Broome, the entire bloody bike rack had somehow bounced off the tyre that supported it. The safety rope had dragged the lot – four bikes and the bike rack itself - along a gravel road for half a mile or so until we noticed. My burnished and buffed new bike was, of course, on the bottom, bravely shielding the decrepit kid's bicycles above it from any damage. How heroic of it.

The quote to fix my bike that I had never ridden: $230. The experience: priceless.

The road on which my new bicycle had been so traumatised ran north from Broome to our next destination, Middle Lagoon. Middle Lagoon was a coastal aboriginal community that took in campers in much the same way as the cattle stations. It was a beautiful place, and was friendly and sensibly run.

To imagine Middle Lagoon, start with any naturally stunning bay that you can think of: let's say Bondi Beach in Sydney. Then bulldoze all buildings, and banish the roads. Now build a tranquil bush campsite overlooking the beach. Have the sun set over that beach every evening, followed by a billion stars lighting up the night sky. Plonk a quietly spoken

Aboriginal man behind a desk in a tiny shop to run the place. Then you'll have Middle Lagoon.

The only other major difference between these other beautiful beaches and Middle Lagoon - and it's a vital one - is that you'd have *the whole place to yourself*. You can swim for an hour in the clear turquoise water, or walk the kilometre or so to the other end of the bay, without sighting another person. Imagine doing *that* at Bondi.

Our campsite sat atop a high sand ridge, directly overlooking the ocean. Thus it lent itself admirably to sunset watching, becoming an obvious spot for evening drinkies. This was an easy habit to get into. After a couple of lazy days at Middle Lagoon, swimming in the idyllic bay, and walking along the idyllic beach, we headed off in the Jackaroo to explore the rest of the peninsula. We'd heard that the northern tip, named Cape Leveque, was well worth a visit.

"How far to the nearest petrol station Kath?" I asked as we turned out of Middle Lagoon, heading toward the cape, which was about 100km distant. This simple question initiated a chain of events that, shall I say, distracted us for a while.

Kath decided that there would almost certainly be petrol at Cape Leveque – it was, after all, the major attraction in the area. We continued merrily along the road. Half an hour later, with the indicator needle on the petrol tank heading steadily toward the 'E', I became nervous. We consulted a map to check for garages. Cape Leveque did not, unfortunately, have a little green petrol tank symbol next to it. However a small Aboriginal community named Lombardina, about 20km back, did have that important little icon. So rather than risk driving onward, we backtracked to Lombardina, and were heartened to see a sign advising "seven day petrol" at the community entrance.

If I had a tin of paint with me, I would have stopped at that sign on the way out and added the words "except on Sunday". Sure, the community had a petrol bowser, but it was padlocked. We tried to find someone to unlock it, but the entire community seemed to be asleep, even though it was well after 10am. I had a mosey around the deserted community – it was a spooky feeling, like wandering around an aboriginal ghost town - and eventually came across a young boy carrying a basketball. He directed me to the house of the tribal elder, whom, he thought, probably had the key.

The house to which he directed me seemed to have been abandoned for at least a year. The kid was either geographically challenged or had an ultra-ultra-dry sense of humour.

After another 15 minutes or so of aimless loitering, I spotted an elderly man – a white man - pottering about his back yard. I ambled over and said gidday. From his accent, it was immediately clear that he was German. And it was very quickly evident that he was undoubtedly of the Crazy kind. Oh no.

I burned with curiosity to discover how an elderly German came to be living in a remote aboriginal community, but, after listening to his doddering, rambling greeting for a minute, instead quickly focused upon our petrol problem. He responded with 10 minutes of unrelated observations on the mornings' weather, during which I could barely interject with any observations of my own. Finally, I managed to steer his reply back to our original problem of the locked petrol bowser, to which he responded with a further 10 minutes of incomprehensible directions to the house of someone whom he thought might help us. I had already decided that I was not going to bother even trying when he added "but zay proobably vont be avake vor a vew hours...." I quickly retreated to the safety of the car before he tried to help us again.

I think these aboriginal communities are onto a good thing. It would be about noon before anyone awoke. Noon! Note well, all you workaholics.

After this disappointment, I capitulated. Goodness knows how much longer it might take to find the possessor of the mystical petrol pump key – it could be hours. Or days. Not wanting to waste more time on ghost houses or blithering Germans (but I admit I am still very curious as to how he came to be living at a remote coastal aboriginal community) we decided to try our luck at Cape Leveque. An hour after we left it, we were finally back to our previous turnaround point, but now with 40 km less fuel in the tank. We pointed the Jackaroo northward, and ploughed determinedly forward.

Somehow, we missed the turnoff for Cape Leveque. May I add, at this point, that my job was to hold the steering wheel and point the car in the direction indicated by my *navigator*, who had the *map*, the *brochures* and all of the *information regarding petrol stations* at her disposal.

We inadvertently continued along the northern road, and soon ended up on the uppermost tip of the peninsula in another Aboriginal community called One Arm Point. The petrol gauge was now below empty. Were we going to be stuck here, like a one-armed man hanging off a bridge?

However, we all gave a huge sigh of relief, and I sarcastically congratulated Kath on stuffing up the road directions, when we spied a petrol station. We were saved.

But our relief was very short lived. These bowsers required a pre-purchased petrol card, which, of course, we did not have. The community's only shop was nearby; unsurprisingly but very frustratingly, it was closed. I'm guessing the proprietors were asleep.

We couldn't drive further; we couldn't risk driving back in hope. We were effectively stranded.

In desperation, we puttered around in circles inside the community, and eventually encountered a friendly young couple who were, for some unknown reason, awake. They told us that the reception at Cape Leveque campground sold fuel cards. This information at least gave us some firm direction, rather than the guesswork on which we had been relying thus far.

However, the camp ground was at least 20 km back down the road, and our petrol tank was now suffering acute dehydration.

Bereft of other options we drove, very slowly, back in the direction from whence we came. I even resorted to shifting into neutral gear and coasting down any downhill sections in the belief that it would use less fuel. It was with great relief that we spotted the turnoff to Cape Leveque – how the navigator had *blatantly missed it* on the way through I will never know – and we chugged into the camp reception.

The young lady attending the desk informed me that petrol cards were $25 each. Once swiped through the bowser, they would provide us with 10 litres of fuel each. Furthermore, we were strictly limited to two cards.

Two? I did some quick maths. (Kath was so proud.) Two cards would give us 20 litres, which would take us about 100 km down the road. But it was 80 km back to Lombardina, where this shemozzle had started, and a further 40 km back to camp.

Beaut. Just bloody beaut. We had driven forward and backward, and would now have to drive backward and forward again, just to get back to where we had been. And we'd then be out of petrol again!

I turned my charm up to "schmooze", and dialled my earnest look to "beg". A minute later, I was the proud owner of THREE fuel cards – enough to get us back to camp, where our fuel tins sat waiting for us on the trailer. We re-headed back to the bowser at One Arm

Point, hoping that the petrol fumes remaining in our tank would last the distance.

The fuel gauge was now so far left it was turning communist. A red light on the dashboard was glowing, which, according to the Jackaroo service manual, meant "stop driving immediately, you dickhead, and get some petrol." So it was with complete relief – we had now covered 60km since the gauge first indicated it was completely empty– that we pulled up to the bowser, and filled the car with 30 litres of precious fuel.

$2.50 per litre? Cheap at twice the price.

By now we were feeling too stressed to bother with much exploration of the Cape. Instead, we treated ourselves to takeaway lunch at the Cape Leveque café, and headed back to Middle Lagoon to make an early start on the afternoon drinks. We'd achieved nothing, seen nothing, and had effectively driven about 300km for hamburgers and chips. But it felt good to be back next to the warmth, comfort and security of our petrol canisters.

Just before finishing our tale of that Sunday, I'd like to recount something we saw on the final stretch into camp that was quite arresting. But before I extrapolate, I'd like you to quickly do something for me: just picture a place that is about 1.5 kilometres from your house.

Got it? Just mentally pick somewhere a mile or so from your house. Good.

We were on the way back to camp when, by the side on the road, we saw a young aboriginal girl. She was about two years old, and as cute as a button – brown hair, massive brown eyes, bare-footed, and wearing a little denim skirt and a pink top. We slowed up so that we didn't cover her with dust, and as we passed her, she gave us a little wave and a big smile.

We slowed to a stop. We looked around but could not see any adults, or even older children. Not even a dog. The little girl waved and smiled again, but said little. We hadn't passed civilisation of any sort for at least five kilometres. What on earth was a tiny young girl doing so far from anywhere by herself?

We tried to establish where she was from – Where's home? Where's mummy or daddy? - but we could not get any answers out of her. After a few minutes, we could do nothing but drive onward to camp, awkward with the feeling that we had abandoned a baby girl in the middle of nowhere.

We later established that the young girl had wandered out from Middle Lagoon. She had walked – no, toddled – about 1.5 kilometres to where we had spotted her, before eventually tottering her own way back later that afternoon. Nobody at camp had noticed that she was missing.

Now just imagine that you have a two-year-old daughter. (Maybe you do.) Now contemplate the possibility of her wandering independently to your previously imagined point, a mile away from your house, and eventually returning home – all without you noticing that she was gone. Scarily unlikely.

I'd love to tell you the significance of this, but I haven't figured it out yet myself. Is it a wonderful reflection on the freedom of living in a remote community, or is it a damning insight into lax parenting?

Maybe the old Crazy German man from Lombardina could tell us both. Please ask him if you're ever passing through. Just allow yourself an hour or so for the answer.

Chapter Nine: The West Kimberley

After leaving the Broome Peninsula (straying only for the aforementioned repair to my new bicycle) we headed east toward Derby. It was a welcome change to be heading on a bearing other than north – after driving for so long every morning in the same direction, we were all getting suntanned on just one side of our faces.

I was looking forward to visiting the Kimberley, the northern region of WA, with keen anticipation. It had been the focus of my attention since Kath had originally begged me to take the family on this entire tour. I could barely contain myself when we woke up in Derby, the gateway town to the Kimberley, and hitched up the ol' camper trailer. A couple of weeks in this remote and rugged wilderness awaited.

However, Kath and the kids weren't bursting at the seams to undertake the 650km dirt-road drive quite as much as I was. They ganged up on me and decided, by a vote of 4-1, to visit the Derby School of the Air before we left. The School of the Air teaches those kids who, due to their geographical isolation - such as living in remote communities or pastoral stations - can't make it to a bricks-and-mortar school. They do most of their lessons via shortwave radio, and, more recently, over the internet.

The tour was *reeeally* fascinating. We saw the stationery cupboard, some computers, the sports equipment locker and the teachers' desks. We even got to meet the principal. Wow! I was absolutely gutted when - halfway through the tour, just before we were about to see the P&C committee meeting room - I remembered that I had to make an urgent phone call* and politely excused myself.

Sorry, I'm being overly-facetious here. The tour was better than I have depicted, but my big sister Maria once worked for the School of the Air in the outback town of Longreach, so I was already familiar with the basics of the operation. We actually did get taken to the stationery cabinet for 20 minutes though, I kid you not. Nevertheless, Kath and the kids found it very worthwhile. The tour also scratched Kath's teacher itch, which was feverishly irritating her after a month out of the classroom.

The Kimberly School of the Air teaches students who live over an area of 450 000 km^2. I know that you weren't really paying attention when you read that last sentence, so I'll say the important bit again. *450 000 km^2*. That's a bloody big area for a school catchment zone. To put this figure in some perspective: if this school zone were a country, it would rank, on size, as the 56th largest on the planet, out of 255 countries. It dwarfs Germany (348 000 km^2) and Japan (364 000 km^2). It is almost twice the size of the United Kingdom, which measures a comparatively paltry 242 000 km^2.

Despite being so geographically large, the Kimberly School of the air caters for less than 100 students,

---

* The urgent call was to see how my mum had fared at golf the previous week.

which highlights the sparse population density in this corner of the planet. Imagine, if you would, a school that covered all of Germany yet had only a few dozen pupils. Yet these hardy souls get together every month or so for assessment, sports days, social interaction, or whatever other activities are best done together rather than apart. Sometimes, particularly in wet season, the school has to send a helicopter to pick up the students, for the roads are often impassable.

Suddenly having to catch the bus home from school each day as a kid didn't seem like such a big impost.

Our last stop on the way out of Derby was a quirky little tourist attraction called the Boab Jail Tree. Boabs, with their huge water–storing capacity, are the camels of the Kimberley. Their trunks are massive, up to five metres in diameter, and can hold a small swimming pool full of water. They are native to, and synonymous with, the Kimberley region. This particular tree was very large, and had a conveniently hollow centre, forming a room-sized cavity. In the early 1900s, a steel door was added to the open side of the cavity, transforming the tree into an overnight watch-house for prisoners being marched from the bush into Derby for trial.

A tree for a jail? Only in the Kimberley. I tried to lock the kids up for a while – just to smarten them up a bit - but unfortunately they are all now faster than I am.

After visiting the jail-tree, I finally got my wish. We turned left out of Derby and hit the Gibb River Road – a rocky dirt track that runs straight through the guts of the Kimberley - and we headed bush.

We had heard and read a lot about the Gibb River Road before undertaking the trip: this rough bush track had teeth, and ate cars for breakfast. We had heard numerous tales of motorists being stranded for days after the track had shredded their spare tyres; of caravanners picking up bits of broken axle after taking a dip too quickly; of motor homes being swept away while traversing river crossings. The track didn't disappoint.

At first, the Gibb River Road was just bumpy, but then became progressively rockier. Steadily the stones got larger and larger until we were virtually driving over boulders. Razor sharp flints lay scattered across the tracks, ready to rip your tyres to shreds should you take your eyes off the road for even a second. Some of the river crossings were a metre deep - and they were the good sections. The bad patches, well, even the kangaroos feared to cross them.

I'm sorry, but I have deceived you yet again. The description above is not really of the Gibb River Road, but is what I was told the Gibb River Road would be like. In reality, the Gibb was a well-graded bush track, not much different from what you'd find a couple of hours from any capital city. Sure, it had a few rocky patches and creek crossings to keep it interesting, but it was nothing like we had heard.

It seems common among travellers to tell everyone else how horrific the roads are. I suppose it gives the teller an inflated feeling of conquest – sort of like exaggerating the size of the fish that got away.

What the Gibb River Road *did* have was corrugations – lots of them. It felt like we were driving on the roof of an old tin shed. The insidious little bumps made your car, and everything in it, shake, rattle and roll. We'd usually arrive at our destination to discover that screws, nuts and bolts had unwound out of each other – a panel would fall off the camp fridge, a handle would separate from a pot, fillings would fall from your teeth, that sort of thing.

I must admit, however, that I was surprised when, at the end of a long drive along the Gibb, I opened up a tub of cream to find that it had turned into butter.

OK, I made that last bit up too. But it *was* bumpy.

The other thing the Kimberley had lots of was dust. Bulldust. These tiny, fine particles of red dirt filled the air, and somehow navigated their way into the most improbable places. For example, the dust would work its way into the back of the car, then into a zippered-up bag. From there it would traverse through all of your clothes, and bypass another zipper on your toiletry bag, before somehow shimmying into a sealed container and settling on your toothbrush. Everything, and everybody, was permanently covered in a light dusting of red ochre.

Even though it may sound disgusting, the dirt and dust are not as annoying as you might imagine. Because the dust is so fine, it's not gritty, so even though you look like you've just tumbled down Uluru, you don't *feel* dirty. And the air is so dry that the dust sits lightly on your skin, rather than getting grimy. I liked to think of it as bush talcum powder. Or an instant Kimberley tan.

I'm sure there's a beauty clinic somewhere that would make a fortune selling tubs of the stuff with a little powder-puff brush.

We learnt a couple of tricks to cope with the conditions up here in the Kimberley , which might come in handy should you ever decide to undertake such a venture yourself. First, squish a little blob of blu-tack, or similar substance, onto the ends of all the bolts – for example, the roof rack fixings. The tacky substance prevents the nuts from rattling loose and disappearing into the roadside dust forever. You can even use old chewing gum.

Second, when driving along particularly dusty roads, turn your car's air conditioning fan to its highest setting. This has the effect of creating a positive air pressure inside your car, meaning that the air seeps *out* the cracks rather than blowing in. Because air is continuously trickling out of the nooks and crannies, the dust cannot get in as readily. Some of it will – that stuff has miraculous powers of navigation through even the tiniest of gaps – but you will lessen its impact.

Our first Kimberley stopover was at Windjana, one of many gorges that dot the area. After setting up camp, we ambled off to explore. Soon we came across the ranger station, which was filled with signs displaying useful information. It's good to get advice from the experts *before* you do something stupid that you didn't realise was dangerous. For example, one prominent sign clearly proclaimed:

FOR YOUR SAFETY, AND FOR THE HEALTH AND WELL BEING OF THE CROCODILES, PLEASE STAY MORE THAN 4 METRES AWAY FROM THEM.

Well thank you, Captain Obvious! Was it *really* necessary to warn people to stay four metres away from Mother Nature's all-time most ruthlessly efficient killing machine? And as for "the health and wellbeing of the crocodiles" … they can't be serious. What were we going to do if we got closer? Bite them? If ever there is an award for "most useless sign ever" then this one deserves the gong.

We duly set off into the gorge, and soon encountered a bask of crocodiles. (Yes, bask is the collective noun for crocodiles.) There were probably two dozen or more reptiles just lying there in the sun, like deadwood. As the sign suggested, we kept our distance. Plenty of distance.

After a while, we wanted more action. Come on crocs, shouldn't you be attacking something? You know, dragging a passing wallaby into the creek, or lunging out of the water to drag a small defenceless mammal off an overhanging branch. Or at least having a crack at the kids.

However, no, they all just lay there in the sun. And believe it or not, we began to creep closer to them; first 15 metres, then ten. Still, they didn't move. As we got closer, it became clear that these were freshwater crocodiles, which are naturally small. And these were just young 'uns. They were kind of, well, cute.

So, believe it or not, the boys and I crept to within a few metres of the crocs, ironically defying what, just half an hour earlier, I had felt was the most unnecessary advice I had ever been given by an inanimate object. Our proximity to the crocs terrified Kath and Caity, who subsequently spent the next half an hour hollering at us to get back, but at the same time retreating, thereby making their exhortations easily ignorable.

Whenever we closed to within four or five metres, the little cuddly toy crocodiles would slide into the water and swim away. I must admit it gave me a mild tingle of satisfaction to know that *they* were scared of *me*. Steve Irwin, the late, great crocodile hunter, would be spinning in his grave if he could read this hubris. I'm sorry Steve, I know they were only freshies, but a guy has to start developing his croc machismo somewhere.

After we had finished gently taunting the crocs, we continued our waltz up the middle of Windjana Gorge. It had one feature that distinguished it from the other gorges we had seen thus far: its height. Windjana has some really colossal walls, which at some points rose a dizzying 200 metres. I couldn't believe that this place was not the global headquarters for the Rock Climbing Lunatics Association, the Crazy-arsed Base Jumpers Society, or Abseilers Anonymous.

That afternoon we took a drive to the other notable local attraction, Tunnel Creek. As astute readers may remember, one's torch must be of a certain sufficient standard to be of use to oneself at Tunnel Creek. So, just to spite the old bat who had irritated me at

114

Karijini, we not only took all six of our torches, but also a couple of head-lights, a big fluoro lamp, some candles, a couple of boxes of matches and a transistor radio with a nice bright LED as well.

OK, I admit that this would not have irritated the old bat at all. She was about 3000 km away, probably haranguing some backpacker for being younger than she was. But it did make me feel better.

We'd heard that Tunnel Creek was great fun to explore, so we were all anticipating this adventure keenly. We skidded to a halt in the car park, which was deserted, except for two tour buses. We skipped excitedly through the twisting ravines that led to the cave's entrance, and then paused to allow a couple of grey nomads, who were clambering out of the rock-strewn tunnel entrance, to pass. We were about to enter when we spied another few oldies, and again we retreated to give them free passage. Mistake. Big mistake.

It was soon clear that these people were merely the vanguard of a tour group of about 30 dear, friendly, but agonisingly slow, oldies. So we waited patiently as they stepped ever so gingerly through the rocky entrance. They were unfailingly polite, but gee, it took them a long time.

Every so often we'd politely enquire how many of the party were still to come, and were heartened to hear that the number was gradually shrinking. Finally, one dear old lady reported that she was among the slowest in her group, and that the rearguard would be along presently.

But still they kept appearing, like ants out of a mound, seemingly endless in supply. After ten more interminable minutes, we enquired again as to how many of the party were to come.

"Oh, probably still about 20 or 30 – some of them are a bit old, you know," came the reply. It dawned on us that this was now the group from the second bus, which had merged seamlessly with the first mob. So again, we waited, exchanging pleasantries with the seniors, for most of the rest of the afternoon. I'd even go so far as to say that our wait outside Tunnel Creek put public service help-line response times to shame.

With the patience that only comes from having nothing pressing in our schedule for two months, we sat. Finally, our turn came. I'm desperately trying to come up with a line here other than "it was worth the wait", but I just can't think of one. So: It was worth the wait.

For 800 metres, we waded and walked our way through this underground tunnel, which was lit handsomely ablaze by our sufficient array of torches. Large stalactites poked down threateningly from the ceiling, while in other places dozens of smaller ones formed inverted beds of nails. It was simultaneously stunning and spooky, eerie and exciting. It was an experience to remember.

We'd heard that a crocodile had recently taken up residence in the dark waters of Tunnel Creek. This concerned many travellers, but not us. The little wimp was only a freshie. Bring it on, I say. Bring it on.

The far end of Tunnel Creek opened onto a sunlit little river. We clambered off in search of an aboriginal art site that we had heard was painted on a cliff face nearby. We were stopped in our tracks by an indignant Aboriginal ranger, who seemed mightily pissed off that we had dared to wander upon his tribe's sacred ground.

I wanted to point out the complete lack of signage, direction or other notification to this effect. I also wished to inform him that other people had recently made this trip in order to inform us about it, so we weren't on our Pat Malone in this regard. What was more, I felt that he should be encouraging people like us (ignorant, white) to view, and therefore develop respect, for such treasured icons, rather than excluding and therefore irritating us. However, I sensed that this information would just prolong the exchange - either that, or this trip was making me too mellow for my own good – so we retreated without argument.

Once we had done Windjana Gorge and Tunnel Creek, (Don't you hate that phrase "done"? I promise I won't use it again - I just put it in there so I could remark on how much I dislike it.) there was little else to see in the area. We had already paid for two nights, so we spent the next day throwing rocks at crocodiles.

No, we didn't really. But we did talk to an aboriginal ranger – not the same boofhead who had turned us away from the art works the day before, but a nice one - who told us the story of Jandamarra. Back in the 1890s, the local police regarded a local aboriginal man called Jandamarra as the best tracker around. Their opinion of him was so high that they employed him, with immediate success; he and his police partner Richardson became the dynamic duo of local law enforcement. Jandamarra was instrumental in capturing a notorious group of thieves. Unfortunately, he soon realised that one of the gang members was his uncle.

Jandamarra's family ties held him more tightly than did his loyalty to his employer, so he released the prisoners and headed bush with them, killing his police partner and stealing a cache of guns as he did. Suddenly, he was not quite the darling of the police set, and they issued a warrant for his arrest. Later, Jandamarra caused further angst when he killed two cattle drovers. Soon thereafter, a posse of 30 heavily armed men set out to capture him.

So far, Jandamarra's story was little more than a tale of a talented but ratbag thief who got himself into a lot of trouble and then fled to the hills. However, as the search for Jandamarra continued his legend grew, for he seemed uncatchable. Despite 30 men scouring the hills around Windjana gorge, he seemed to leave no trace of his travels. On many occasions, after each of his hit-and-run-missions, the large constabulary thought that they had cornered Jandamarra in a rocky gully. Yet somehow he seemed to evaporate into thin air. Rumours grew that he was from the spirit world, and that he could not be caught by a white man.

Jandamarra's big advantage was his local knowledge of the land. What he knew — and what his pursuers didn't – was of the existence of Tunnel Creek. Whenever the law was closing in on him, he would scurry into the mountain ranges that surround this natural underground pipeline. Then he would skirt through the unseen portal and emerge on the other side of the mountain, far away from his confounded chasers.

Each time that he escaped from his captors, Jandamarra's legend grew. He became an outlaw hero, particularly amongst his own tribe, the Bunuba people. They regarded him as almost godlike – a manifestation of the spirit in the water of Tunnel Creek.

Ultimately, Jandamarra was caught. Just as the legends foretold, he was not captured by a white man, but by an aboriginal tracker called Micki from a rival tribe. Jandamarra was shot just outside the Tunnel Creek entrance, no doubt attempting his usual escape route. Yet his legend lives on, and to this day, the locals love to tell the story of Jandamarra.

*

Do you remember that 1980s movie entitled *Blue Lagoon*? It starred a youthful and gorgeous Brooke Shields, and a very lucky young actor named Christopher Atkins. The movie, which was set in the stunningly beautiful, idyllic surrounds of the eponymous Blue Lagoon, was a story of young teenagers discovering their sexuality. Well, at least I think that was the theme. I was too busy trying to catch a glimpse of Brooke's titties to follow the plot.

I think it is time for a remake of this movie. It would be called *Blue Lagoon II – The menopausal years*. The story would explore, in depth, the sexual proclivities of a 40-ish-year-old couple trapped together in an impossibly beautiful setting. In the lead female role would be Angelina Jolie. The male role would be filled by, let's say, me.

The reason that I have inserted one of my fantasies into a travel book is that I have found the location for such a cinematic masterpiece. In fact, I have found two places, should they need certain scenes, er, re-shot.

These two impossibly wondrous places, whose splendour surpasses anything that the fictional Blue Lagoon can dish up, were our next two stops along the Gibb River Road. They were named, respectively, Bell Gorge and Manning Gorge.

Looking every bit like a movie set visual cliché, these gorges featured deep crystal-clear blue water, surrounded by fortress-like walls of rich red sandstone. A gushing waterfall tumbled into each lagoon, and then cascaded down mini-falls further downstream, before settling once again into the job of being a Kimberley creek.

If the wonderful surrounds (and the Angelina Jolie fantasy) weren't enough to lift your spirits, then the fun that you could have swimming certainly was. Even though it was the middle of winter, Kimberley days reach about 28 degrees or so. The water temperature was just perfect for a refreshing dip.

When you tired of lazy swimming, there were waterfalls to swim under, further streams and pools to explore, and cliffs off which to jump. The kids and I scrambled our way up a rocky gorge wall, about three metres or so above the waterline. After a few minutes of nervous motivation and cajoling, we each mustered up the courage to leap, and hit the cool water with four large splashes, although I concede one of the splashes was a little larger than were the others.

This should have been enough. However, some young backpackers had arrived, and were audaciously leaping off a ledge far higher up the cliff face. After watching them having a great time for 15 minutes, I thought that I'd join them. It looked only about eight or nine metres high, but hey, Olympians *dive* from higher than that, and not only add some twists and turns on the way down, but enter the water head first as well. I just wanted to do a simple, feet-first jump. How hard could it be?

With a flow of discouraging words from Kath ringing in my ears, I picked my way up the cliff face. After ascending to the platform, I looked over the edge to the water below – way, *way* below – and instantly knew that I had made a mistake. I just could not fathom how a cliff that looked less than 10 metres high from the side, had miraculously transformed, as I scaled it, into a towering fortress at least twice that height. Suddenly, the water looked very distant, and very, *very* hard.

Permit me at this point to establish some of my macho credentials regarding heights. I am not a complete scaredy cat. I have parachuted from 40 000 ft, bungee jumped in New Zealand, and even powered a solo flight via a jet pack, tethered only by a 90 metre long cable. However, looking down at that distant, hard, black water, I have to admit I was terrified.

Too terrified. I couldn't do it. I turned around, and, with shame burning in my ears, I slowly climbed my way back down the cliff.

As if. Did you believe me? I hope not. Rather, I steeled myself again, relaxed my mind with a series of Zen-like deep breathing manoeuvres, and, before any more negative thoughts could ruin the moment for me again, I jumped. I hit the water within milliseconds. Amidst a cloud of bubbles and broken water, I managed to swim back up to the surface only 10 minutes later - that's how long it felt, anyway.

Naturally, I felt pleased with myself for overcoming my fears. I also gained massive new respect for Olympic high divers. And a very clean pair of nostrils.

By the time we departed Manning Gorge we were about 350km along the Gibb. Our nights in the Kimberley so far had been spent at rough bush camps. These have many advantages – you can cook your dinner on a camp fire, for one – and they were very quiet and private. However, after a week or so of dust, I could sense that Kath and Caitlin, in particular, were pining for civilisation. But we still had about 350 km of the Gibb River Road to traverse before we would reach anything resembling developed society. So despite the girls' wishes, we had little choice but to head that night for another station bush camp called Home Valley.

As we rounded the bend into Home Valley, eight eyeballs (specifically, those of Kath and the kids) nearly hit the floor. This place was green, not red. It had lawn, not dust. And there was a huge, spanking new adventure playground! There was a pool! And a shower block! The buzz in the car was palpable as we pulled up at reception.

I was just trying to calm the rest of the family down and to restore some order to the excitable rabble when I spied the bar. A huge bar, with beer on tap, pretty barmaids, and a band playing on a corner stage. Now *my* eyeballs hit the floor. Whoooo–hooooeeee!

Unbeknownst to us (and our guidebooks), Home Valley had just spent a cool $21 million on refurbishments. Yes, you read that correctly: twenty one million dollars. That kind of money buys some seriously good camp site facilities, trust me. The new site had only been reopened for six days, and hence was new, fresh, clean, and sparkling. It was so new that even the stable floors were shit-free. We were all very happy indeed.

The movie *Australia*, featuring Nicole Kidman and Hugh Jackman, had been filmed in and around Home Valley a year or so previously, and was about to be released. The upcoming publicity had been the spur to spend big bucks, to hopefully cash in on the movies' success.

That night we left the camp oven in its shelf and treated ourselves to a three-course meal at the huge, open-air restaurant. After that, we huddled around the communal campfire, where a professional didgeridoo player called Mick held court. Lachie took a particular shine to the didgeridoo and picked up the basics pretty quickly. Somehow he even mastered the art of circular breathing, which is an aboriginal-developed skill of breathing out through your mouth and in through your nose at the same time, enabling a didgeridoo player to continue with a note indefinitely. I tried to follow Mick's instructions but I simply could not grasp the concept. Try it yourself if you're thinking I'm a bit of a dill.

Later, as we hustled the children off to bed, Mick offered to give the kids another didgeridoo lesson the next day. The next morning we duly took him up on his offer, and within half an hour Lachie was playing the didge like a born-and-bred blackfella. Mick even loaned him an instrument so that he could practice for the rest of our stay.

We had only intended Home Valley to be a quick one-night stopover, but ended up staying for three. We spent some happy times just doing simple things —four wheel driving and hiking the local gorges and swimming holes, and trying to wear the kids out by sending them over an obstacle course on the adventure playground for a couple of hours straight. We even had a pony ride.

I also attempted to catch barramundi from the nearby river, but landed only catfish. I was starting to think that catching a barra was not just elusive but impossible. Perhaps, I thought, I should pick another dream to chase.

On our second day, the crew from a popular television travel show called *Getaway* arrived to do a story on Home Valley. They filmed a mini-muster in which the local jackaroos, plus a bloke called Dermott Brereton, a famous footballer-turned-TV-presenter, were on horseback, trying to drive a herd of cattle into the containing yard. However, they were obviously out of practice – in fact I don't think any of them had *ever* mustered on horseback before – and the cattle kept breaking away. Amidst much frustration and cussing, they would then round up the herd again, and then re-attempt to drive them through the paddock gates. Invariably the lead beasts would baulk, and the whole herd would scamper for the scrub again.

After eight or nine re-takes, they finally managed to coax about a dozen cows into the yard, and decided that enough was enough. So if you ever watch a re-run of *Getaway* and you see Dermie Brereton astride a horse, spouting out the words "that was a lot of work, but a heap of fun" you'll know it's been muttered between gritted teeth.

On our last morning at Home Valley a new mob of campers pulled up in the site next door. After chatting for a while, they mentioned that they were heading west, toward Derby. I fulfilled my traveller's duty by warning them about the fiendishly rough and dangerous Gibb River Road. Did they have at least three spare tyres? The rocks were sharp, and ate cars for breakfast. And watch that those creek crossings don't wash your trailer away....

I drove off toward the looming bitumen with a wry grin on my face.

Chapter Ten: The Bungle Bungles

After leaving Home Valley, we continued along the Gibb River Road until its end, thus drawing to a close, for a while, this chapter of our adventure. I say "for a while" because I had pre-booked to stay in a resort at El Questro station, which is next door to Home Valley, in a few days' time. This commitment, our only firm pre-booking on the entire tour, was to coincide with Kath's birthday.

We calculated that we had three nights in the Bungles if we were to make it back to the resort by then. So we left the Gibb, turned right, and headed south down the highway to the Bungle Bungles – otherwise known as - and I think I've spelled this right - Purnulululululu National Park.

Like the Gibb River Road, we had heard many horror stories about the track into the Bungles. But like the Gibb, they were exaggerated. Sure, the road had lots of twists and turns, seven creek crossings, and some deep washouts, but it was fun – like an automobile version of a roller coaster.

Plenty of people obviously felt it was a tough drive, as you could buy a bumper sticker at the rangers' office that read "I survived the drive into the Bungle Bungles." Not a bad idea. Maybe I'll start a range of "I survived..." stickers. For example "I survived the Crocs at Windjana", "I survived the jewellery shops in Broome" or – and this one is bound to be a big seller - "I survived the German backpackers at Pardoo Station".

The Bungle Bungles is a range of striped, domed mountains, scattered with gorges and chasms. The domes are 'outback red' in colour, permeated with purple and brown horizontal bands. Some say that these mountains look like giant scoops of ice cream. Others say that they look like colossal Christmas puddings, while others imagine gigantic jelly moulds. To me it is clear that they resemble a series of extremely large breasts. Oh, come on, stop pretending that you hadn't already thought of that yourself.

The unique charm of the place led it to being World Heritage Listed in 2003. Bizarrely, the entire mountain range – over 2000 hectares of natural wonders – wasn't 'discovered' until 1983, just two decades earlier. Of course, the ranges had been there for 200 million years, give or take a few hours, but nobody was paying them much attention. Some aboriginal tribes called part of it home, while the rest was a cattle station. The station owners thought the mountains were a nuisance, except for a few rare places where they formed a natural cattle yard, saving the farmer a few bob on fencing. It is staggering that the Bungles have gone from complete obscurity to being a world famous landmark in such a short space of time.

The unique rocks and interesting landscapes of the park naturally leant themselves to bushwalking, so that's what occupied most of our time in the Bungles. We took two nice walks on the first day, and another pair on the second day. These hikes included Echidna Chasm; we didn't see any echidnas, but we have a great time exploring this freakish gorge. Its walls are over 100m high, yet are so close that you could touch them simultaneously with outstretched arms.

The lack of wind or fire in these chasms encouraged the evolution of a species of palm unique to the Bungles. Due to their protected position these palms grow to magnificent heights, to my eye about 50 metres, but have trunks that are so impossibly thin that you could wrap your fingers around them.

Before the trip began, I expected that most of our travelling compatriots would be of the retired variety, but I nonetheless thought that we would encounter other families similar to ours every few days. Not so. In fact, we had encountered very few families on the road at all. It was with some joy that, on our second morning at The Bungles, we spied another family – a real mum and dad, a girl about Caitlin's age, and a young boy about Jake's age – setting up camp nearby. We quickly made friends, and spent the ensuing evenings in each other's company. Although Kath and the kids are excellent company, it was nice to have a few fresh faces around the campfire. My lot had already heard my Pardoo fishing stories many times and were tiring of them; this new audience were enraptured as I described the thrill of my massive catches, and later added the standard rejoinder about the dangerous roads as well.

Our other little adventure in the Bungles was a short joy-flight helicopter ride to view this spectacular range from the air. Each 'copter could only take three passengers, so I was resigned that we'd have to book two separate flights, and was prepared to cop the concomitant hit to my wallet. However, Kath politely declined the offer on the basis that she could think of nothing worse.

I tried, I really tried, to talk Kath into joining us on the joy flight. But she kept interrupting with inane objections like "what if it crashes into a mountain" and "what if the engine conks out in mid air". The fact that the aviation company were accredited, certified, experienced, vetted and compliant with every aeronautical statute did nothing to change her mind. She just couldn't shake the irrational fear that the engines would stall, or that the helicopters would crash into a mountain. In the end, Lachie drew the short straw to stay behind and eat ice cream with Kath, while the rest of us headed off for an aerobatic sight-seeing thrill ride.

Soon Caitlin, Jake and I had donned our aviator sunnies. I nearly looked as big a jerk as did Tom Cruise in *Top Gun*, but not quite. Minutes later, we were dizzily whirring a few hundred metres above the national park.

For some reason these helicopters had no doors, so the only thing between you and the ground was a terrifyingly thin seat belt. The 'copters were small, and therefore easily bullied by the wind, so you really felt every lurch of turbulence. These features added to the sense of danger and excitement –at no extra cost!

The joy ride also came with a free hair blow-dry. Did you realise that helicopters are windy? I'm sure you did, but I didn't expect it to be hurricane force five.

Between the open cockpit, the helicopter's speed across the ground, and the powerful down draft from the rotors, the wind was so strong that it whipped the screams right out of your mouth before you could hear them.

Like Caity and Jake, I was fairly crapping myself for the first couple of minutes. It was particularly hairy when the pilot did banked turns, exposing you even more acutely to the drop below. After a few minutes I built up my courage, and eventually summoned the nerve to take a few photographs.

My first few shots were hopelessly out of whack. This was due to my reluctance to let go of the hand rail for any longer than a small fraction of a second, lest the pilot suddenly do a big left turn, while my body stayed on its trajectory – straight out the door. It was difficult to point, compose, focus and shoot the picture in 0.001 of a second. Slowly I realised that I wasn't going to fall out of the helicopter, and steadied long enough to take some decent shots.

After an exhilarating 18 minutes, we touched down, feeling awed, excited and, admittedly, just a little pleased to be back on terra firma. No stalled engines, no mountaintop crashes. Off we drove into the sunset, gently taunting Kath for being such an irrational chicken as we did.

*

A week later, we heard on the radio news that a pilot and three young women had taken that same joy flight over the Bungle Bungles. The helicopter's engine stalled in mid air, and it crashed into a mountaintop.

There were no survivors.

Chapter 11: El Questro

We woke up on our third morning in the Bungles. It was Thursday, August 15th - the birthday of one very special mum/wife. We made a fuss over her, and sang an out-of-tune version of *Happy Birthday*. The kids had made her cards the day before, which she received gratefully.

After quickly folding up camp, we drove the 50 km winding road out of the national park and turned back onto the highway. In order to get on the road quickly we hadn't yet had breakfast, so we stopped at Doon Doon roadhouse an enjoyed a birthday brunch for Kath. Despite being in the middle of nowhere (try to find Doon Doon on a map, I challenge you) the feed was excellent, and, for a change, was very reasonably priced.

As an accidental little birthday bonus for Kath, the roadhouse had a television that was showing the Olympic Games. This was the first time we had seen any of the games, and, while we were waiting for our food to arrive, were lucky enough to see the Aussie girls take gold in the swimming relay.

After that interlude we headed north, made a left turn, and soon found ourselves at Emma Gorge, the fancy resort part of El Questro Station. No camper trailer, no tents, and no communal toilet – this was a real resort. It would have bed linen, hot water, and even a bathroom with a mirror. Kath was really looking forward to this 'mini-holiday within a holiday', which was my birthday treat for her.

I entered reception, and introduced myself. The bloke behind the desk, after hearing my name, leafed through a pile of papers, obviously looking for our booking slip. I knew things were not good when he frowned.

"How did you spell your name?"

"P.E.R.R.I.E.R. Perrier."

"Like the water," he joked.

I did my best impression of a chortle.

He leafed through the same pile of papers, then frowned more deeply than the first time. Despite his doubtful body language, I was confident that the booking had been made properly. I had even received an email to confirm it. The date of the booking was also easy to remember– the 15th of August – as it was Kath's birthday.

The bloke then suggested that I wait for the "real" receptionist to return – he was just a barman filling in while she showed some guests to their rooms. I patiently waited, hoping like hell that they hadn't stuffed up. Kath would be gutted if we had to drive off to somewhere else and set up camp again.

Soon enough the real receptionist returned, and I again gave my name. She flicked through the same bunch of papers as the previous guy, and made the same facial gestures.

"When did you have the rooms booked for, Mr Perrier?" she inquired.

"Today. Thursday."

She flicked through the papers again, and frowned again. I was starting to panic a little, which was manifesting as irritation.

"Are you sure about the date?" she asked. We don't seem to have you booked in here tonight."

"Yes", I firmly assured her. "The booking was for today. My wife's birthday. I'm certain. Absolutely certain."

"I seem to remember your name," she said, giving me a glimmer of hope, "but you're not listed here for some reason."

I was losing patience. Surely a world-class resort would have a decent system for accommodation bookings.

"Listen," I said, now a little bit tersely. "There must be some sort of stuff up. I have even received a confirmation e-mail that we were booked in here today. As I said, it's my wife's birthday, so there's no way I would get the date wrong. Thursday the 15th of August."

Suddenly, something seemed to click in her little receptionist brain. She turned around to another pile of papers, and after leafing through them for only a second, pulled one out and held it up. "Ah, here's your booking slip," she said.

I smiled weakly. Surely they were organised enough to keep a piece of paper in the right pile. I hoped that things would improve from here, and that they would be more efficient with dinner bookings and the like.

"But," she said, lowering her tone and looking me in the eye, "while today *is* Thursday, Mr Perrier, unfortunately it is the *14th* of August, not the 15th. I'm afraid that both your booking, and your wife's birthday, are tomorrow."

Kath wouldn't even give the birthday cards back.

In the end, everything worked out well. Luckily, they had two spare cabins into which we booked for the night. (Yes, *two* cabins; the kids couldn't believe their luck that they got to sleep away from mum and dad, all by themselves.) We had a swim, a few drinks, went out for a lovely dinner and retired to bed in a nice cosy cabin.

The next morning I refused on principle to sing "Happy Birthday" to Kath again.

After a big buffet breakfast (at which were obliged, by the Cheapskate Travellers Code of Conduct, to steal bread rolls, ham and cheese for lunch; we smuggled the booty out in Kath's handbag) we headed out in the Jackaroo to explore El Questro Station.

Our first stop was Zebedee Springs. Now I know that sometimes travel monologues such as this must sound like tourist brochures with too many adjectives: wonderful, gorgeous, beautiful, blah blah bloody blah. But with Zebedee springs, I respectfully request that you take your Thesaurus off the shelf, dust it off, look up the word "wonderful" and then apply all its synonyms to Zebedee Springs.

What? You don't have a Thesaurus? Oh, the shame.

Don't worry, I don't either; even if I did, I probably wouldn't know how to use it. But I'm sure you get the idea that Zebedee was a bloody nice place.

The springs are formed where hot water naturally flows out of a rock face and collects in the rock pools below. These pools form a series of hot water baths that are just perfect for lazing around. The water cascades down to the next level, doubling en route as a half-decent shoulder masseuse. About a dozen little pools lie in sequence, each with their own character. The boys even had their first shower for a month.

The whole area is covered by pristine rainforest. Palms dot the edges of the spring, giving Zebedee a cool, tropical feel. The trickling, tumbling sound of the water was soooo soothing, the sky really *was* blue, and the birds really *were* singing in the trees. It was just lovely.

As I lay back in one of the pools, calmly floating in the warm water, I could only think what a wonderful start to Kath's birthday this was.

"This," I thought, "has got to be as relaxing as life can get...."

*

An hour later....

"This," I thought, "has got to be as bloody awful as life can get."

We were in the Jackaroo, heading away from Zebedee Springs toward another of the apparently beautiful gorges in the area. We were half way across a 30

137

metre wide river crossing, creeping along slowly but surely. The water was at a comfortable height, just lapping up to the running boards, when the front left tyre dipped into a rut. Suddenly, without warning or fanfare, the engine stopped. Naturally, I tried to restart it, but the motor wouldn't even turn over.

Not good.

For another few minutes, in a period of steadily escalating anxiety, I kept trying to restart the car. But it steadfastly refused to be coaxed into any other state other than 'dead'. It would not give me the satisfaction of even the tiniest "brrr-rrr-rrr" noise.

So after calmly telling the wife and kids that everything would be all right, I announced, with all the fake bravado I could muster, that I was going to have a look under the bonnet.

I waded to the front of the jackaroo, opened the bonnet, and peered at the array of engine-thingy-bits underneath. I had a suspicion that water had somehow worked its way into one of the components – the fact that we were driving through a river when the engine abruptly conked out was the hint - but I had no idea which part to start tinkering with. Was it the carburettor, the distributor, or the computer? Which bit was the bloody carburettor anyway?

I checked the thermostat. I did this even though I knew for certain that it was not the cause of the problem. I checked the thermostat because, having had trouble with it once before, I knew what it was. I just wanted to feel like I knew what I was doing for a few seconds.

The thermostat looked fine. I poked around for a further five minutes, but could see nothing astray. None the wiser, I decided to try to start it again. Perhaps the water had dried up. I turned the ignition key.

Nothing.

I turned it again, a little more desperately this time. Again, nothing. Not even a tiny click. The engine was dead.

Outside of the Jackaroo the river was lapping at the wheel arches, trickling muddy water in through the door cracks. The rear vision mirror reflected the mortified faces of my three children. In the passenger seat, my wife's taut expression was even more concerning.

"It will be fine, everybody," I lied again. "It's probably just water shorting out the battery." Then I rolled up my shorts in a futile attempt to keep them dry, waded through the waist-deep water to the boot, and then rummaged through a pile of soggy camping gear for the tow rope. It was the only piece of equipment that could help us now.

Then I led my family to the river's edge to wait. We hadn't seen another car all morning. This could take a while….

After a half-an-hour wait that took a month, a vehicle appeared in the distance. We knew that they'd stop to help, not just because of the kind-hearted nature of people in this part of the country, but because our car was in the middle of the creek that they had to cross. They weren't going *anywhere* until they'd helped us out.

We were close enough to the edge of the river that the snatch strap *just* extended to the far bank of the river, so our rescuers could hook us up without having to drive into the river themselves. Small mercies. After a couple of anxious moments in which we appeared not only to be without a running engine, but severely bogged as well, we finally started moving. It was quite a relief to see the Jackaroo on dry land again. Unfortunately, we were now on the far side of the creek. But at least we were out.

I had another authoritative look under the bonnet, but still could not detect anything wrong. Why wouldn't the damn thing turn over? After checking the thermostat a couple more times, I decided to give the ignition one more try. Miraculously, there was a hint of life. I tried again, and was relieved to hear the engine stutter for just a split second longer. Perhaps the water, wherever it had lodged, was drying up. On the third go, the engine gave a bit of a crack, and then spluttered into life. Sure, it was a life that sounded as though it had pneumonia, emphysema and croup, but at least it was alive. Hallelujah!

The engine conked out again a few seconds later, but at least we had hope. At this point our rescuers decided that they'd completed their primary mission –

i.e. getting us out of the way – and headed off down the track.

I wish they'd stayed. I got the car going long enough to turn it around – we had abandoned any thoughts of further exploring, and were now aiming to get to the main centre of El Questro. They had a mechanic there who could hopefully look at (read: fix) it for us. But the longer the engine ran, the sicker it sounded. It was spluttering, coughing and wheezing, and even seemed to sneeze a few times. Perhaps we needed a respiratory physician rather than a mechanic.

Even more worryingly, it seemed to be running only on a few cylinders. I revved it gently for a few minutes, but the problems seemed to be worsening. Nobody was about, and I was anxious to get the car back to some semblance of civilisation. I doubted the engine would go for much longer. Unfortunately, the river crossing was still in our way.

I switched the car off – very reluctantly, as I knew it would be difficult to restart – and waited another 10 minutes. With no guarantee of further help arriving, I decided to attempt the river crossing again. If we got through – and it was a very big IF – then we'd hopefully have enough momentum to get us to the main road, which was only a kilometre or so away. From there we could hopefully flag down some help.

If we didn't get through...ouch.

To lighten the load, Kath and the kids hopped out of the car. I turned the key. The engine spluttered and again kicked into life, but it was sounding very, very sick indeed. The previous spluttering remained, but had been joined by an ominous, jarring, banging sound.

I took a very deep breath, slowly let the clutch out, and dipped the front wheels into the water. Because the engine was so weak, I had to keep the revs extremely high. For the first 10 metres, things progressed as well as could be expected. But then I glanced at the oil pressure gauge. It was plummeting.

This sign, for those who are even more mechanically inept than I, is very, very bad news for an engine. I watched in horror as the dial swept, in the space of a few seconds, from nine, to six, then three, and then zero. A full tank of oil had just totally drained from the engine.

I should not have been surprised at what happened next, but it still caught me unawares. Every warning light on the dashboard suddenly lit up. In a different circumstance, that illuminated, blinking dashboard might even be described as pretty. One that caught my eye was in the centre of the dash, in bright, bold, red lighting. It read: I CAN'T BELIEVE YOU'RE STILL DRIVING, YOU NINCOMPOOP. STOP. STOP NOW! Or words to that effect.

At this stage, I was only half way across the river, but even the car itself was telling me to stop. What is a guy to do? Bereft of alternatives, I took a punt and kept on truckin'. I verbally ordered the engine to keep going, and called it many names, which, if repeated here, would increase the parental guidance rating of this tome to 'X'.

Miraculously, the old girl spluttered, banged and cranked her way up and over the far river bank. As soon as I hit dry land, I switched the engine off – primarily so I wouldn't have to look at those warning lights. They were starting to bug me.

Kath and the kids soon arrived after wading across the stream, and were blissfully unaware of just how serious the problem had become. One last time I started the engine, and for two minutes I drove the most rattling, clattering beast that has moved since Henry Ford turned the first ignition switch. As soon as we hit the main road I switched the engine off, and we coasted down a long hill, in relative peace, for a kilometre.

Before our momentum had even stopped, another car fortuitously appeared in the rear vision. I flagged him down on the fly. He seemed puzzled as to why we needed a tow when we appeared, from his position, to be driving along quite happily. He obliged nevertheless.

As we were dragged into the mechanics in El Questro, my latent mechanical mind was working in overdrive. Obviously there was some internal engine damage – probably a blown head gasket. This was *not* good news: the repair bill could be up to $5000, and it might take a week to fix.

If only.

Chapter 12: El Questro and Kununurra

As we were towed into the central hub of El Questro Station, and despite our unfortunate circumstances, it was difficult not to appreciate what a nice place it was. With a cafe & bar, a steakhouse, tour booking agent, general store and, of course, a mechanic, El Questro central was more like a small town than an old cattle station.

I wandered over to the mechanic's shed to reveal our plight. I took Jake with me as emotional currency; I was prepared to beg, if necessary, for a quick resolution. However, a bushfire had just broken out a few miles away, and all non-essential staff, including the mechanic, had been summoned to man the hoses. He would return, someone guessed, in about four or five hours.

We tried to hitch a ride back to our accommodation at Emma Gorge, just to take some time out to recover from the mornings' mishaps. However, no one was available to give us a lift – they were all out fighting a bushfire for the next, oh, four or five hours. To kill time, we took a champagne river cruise up nearby Chamberlain Gorge. Happy birthday Kath!

On the cruise, we experienced the unusual display of the inhabitant Archer fish. These fish can see above the water line, and when they are hungry they scan the nearby low lying branches. When they spot a tasty morsel – say a cockroach or a fly – they suck in a big mouthful of water, and then spit it, water pistol style, at their unsuspecting prey. If all goes well for the

144

Archer fish, they knock the insect into the water, whereupon it quickly becomes dinner. We had fun taunting the fish with small pieces of bread, and copping a blast of water as retribution.

That night we had yet another dinner as part of the two-day-long festival of Kath's birthday. We deliberately over-imbibed on as much alcohol as we could get our hands on, just to flush away the stress of the day. The next morning, the neural enema had done its trick. After a massive buffet breakfast to further fortify ourselves (this time we stole muffins for lunch), we hitched a lift back to El Questro central to confront the mechanic.

"Oh, the Jackaroo, right," he said laconically. "So you're the dim witted ignoramus who recklessly drove through a creek crossing without first checking the depth, idiotically flooded your motor, and then even more stupidly tried to restart it."

Well, he did not actually say that – but it was clearly what he was thinking. Instead, he simply drawled that we had blown the motor, that he could not help us, and that the best solution was to organise a tow truck 100 km or so to the nearest town, Kununurra. He spoke with the lazy detachment of someone who has seen this engine damage many times before. Later enquiries revealed that this was the truth; dozens of vehicles had suffered a similar fate to ours, one as recently as the day before.

I steadily became more miffed at El Questro station over that creek crossing. In the rough and tumble existence of remote north-western Australia you quickly learn to fend for yourself. We had crossed dozens of creeks and rivers on the trip thus far, and, wherever there had been any doubt, I had done the sensible thing and walked across it first. If you stuff up out here, it is your own fault. But in the hotel that morning, when the receptionist had suggested that we visit Emma Gorge – *it's a really pretty drive* – she had made no mention of the creek crossing that routinely destroyed people's cars, and, ergo, their holidays. Nor were there any signs or depth markers by the creek.

Usually I dislike the way modern life is sanitised to the point of stupidity. Signs and warnings adorn every product or structure in what amounts to nothing more than a massive case of legal arse covering. For example, we once bought a hair dryer that solemnly warned on the label that "this product should not be used while sleeping"; as another example, a bridge that was 100 metres above the surrounding river had a sign saying, "Do not walk on rail." And, can you believe it, someone had installed a sign at Windjana Gorge, instructing you to keep at least four metres away from the crocodiles!

In general I find such unnecessary warnings an irritation, but just this once I wish they had put up a sign saying "deep water crossing" or something similar, rather than sending unsuspecting tourists on a 'pretty drive' to oblivion.

Or maybe I am just looking for someone else to blame.

Two tow trucks were duly arranged – one for the trailer, one for the car. After arriving in Kununurra, we delivered the Jackaroo to the mechanic's premises, set up the trailer, and crashed for the night.

The next morning, the Kununurra mechanic rang. His grave tone foreboded bad news. The verdict: we'd blown four holes, ranging in size from a golf ball to a tennis ball, through of the sides of our engine block. The whole engine needed replacing. We'd also thrown a rod through the centre of the starter motor, completely destroying it.

Repair estimate: $11,000. Time: Two weeks, at least. *If* he could source the parts. Miracle #1: That the car managed to start with such a badly damaged starter motor. Miracle #2: The Jackaroo had managed to drive back across that bloody river! We settled in for a long stay at Kununurra Caravan Park.

The news from the mechanic worsened as each day passed. As he dismantled the engine, he discovered an increasing number of parts that we had destroyed, with the clutch being the most notable omission from the original quote. But the worst part was not the increase in price, it was whenever he uttered the words: "I'll try to get the parts delivered on Friday's truck, but if I can't...."

Because Kununurra is so isolated, the supply truck from Perth only arrived once per week, on a Monday. It departed Perth on Friday, so all deliveries had to be ordered by Wednesday. Therefore, if you ordered a part on a Thursday, you had a 10 day wait until it arrived. Such delays were a simple fact of life out here.

However, there was a plus side to our car problems. Every day, the mechanic called: "John, you'd better come and have a look at this," he would drawl. "I've got to show you why I'm adding another $1000 to your bill." So I'd walk the kilometre around to his workshop, and nod knowingly while he pointed to yet another broken bit that may have come from a tin opener for all I knew. Then I'd walk a kilometre back to camp. Because this little routine occurred nearly every day, I steadily covered about 30 km. I got fitter, lost weight and was feeling terrific.

Until the car broke down, we'd had good fortune on tour: the weather had been almost perfect, we'd had no problems with poisonous insects or other crawly things, no-one had broken vital bones or organs, and we hadn't been mugged, murdered or pillaged. We hadn't even been called any nasty names, although that silly woman at Karijini had disparaged my steak-cooking technique. But as we crossed the Kimberley, fate decided it was time to square the ledger. An old wives' tale says that bad luck happens in threes. I was about to cop the other two.

I received an email from my secretary in Brisbane that simply said "Please phone urgently." Nothing else. Emails like this, you don't need to be told, are never good news.

Before we left on this trip, we had a French student called Helene living with us as an au-pair. She was a nice girl, very tidy and trustworthy, so we agreed that she would house sit while we were away.

At home I had a high-speed internet connection, and paid a hefty $100 per month for unlimited downloads. Being the canny tightwad that I am, I decided to reduce to a minimum data plan while we were away. Using this strategy, I could still check my emails whenever we could get internet access, but it would only cost me $30 per month. Great idea, John! Of course, any excess data use would incur a fee.

When Helene originally moved in, she began using my internet connection. I didn't realise this, and no alarm bells were raised because I had no data limits. Helene, too, was not deliberately stealing – she just assumed (quite correctly at the time) that it was OK. Can you see where this is heading?

After we left, Helene didn't realise that I had changed plans. I saw no reason to inform her as I didn't even know that she relied on my connection. So she, and two of her friends, steadily ran up excess charges on my account.

I was not present at the time, but I would imagine my secretary Sarah's face had a rather shocked expression when she opened the account from Telstra. Helene had inadvertently run up charges of ….

Wait, I want you to guess first. Go on, have a stab. How much excess, in dollar value, do you think she ran up in the first month. Have you had a guess?

Wrong. Try a higher amount.

Ok, I will tell you. It was $7500! Yep, seven thousand, five hundred dollars. Arrgh. In addition, she topped that off with another lazy grand or so in the first three days of the next month before Sarah mercifully put a stop to it.

Now I not only had a car repair bill that had grown to $13000, but also an internet account for $8500. It would have been cheaper for us to take a plane to bloody Paris and stay in a poncy hotel than to camp our way across the Kimberley.

Two bits of bad karma down, one to go. After a week or so in Kununurra, I awoke with a sore throat. The kids and Kath had each suffered from minor viruses in the preceding week, so at first I thought it was more of the same. However, by the third day I could not get out of bed. Every drink felt like it was spiked with shards of glass, and I was swallowing painkillers as if they were beer nuts. My skin burned to the touch with fever and I sweated buckets. I felt desperately weak, and more insipid than a junket sandwich.

As every hour went by, I became weaker and more feverish, until I did not have the strength to roll over in bed. Literally. The diagnosis: bacterial tonsillitis. Being ill when you're away from home is never much fun. In a tent, on hot Kununurra day, it is a sentence in hell.

Think back to the last time you had a raging fever. Can you remember how you lay writhing in bed with the sweat just pouring out of you? All day and night, the sweat just drenched the sheets and doused the pillow. Can you also remember the last time you went summer camping? Imagine that you're lying in the tent on a still day, and it's 37 degrees outside. (Yes, it was 37 degrees in Kununurra, even though it was late spring.) The heat radiated from the tent ceiling like a furnace. The sheets were hot, the pillow hotter. There was not a lick of breeze. It was just hot, bloody hot. You're sweating again, aren't you?

Now, multiply those two sweats together. I sweated so much that a small creek formed outside our tent. I was so feverish that Kath tried to save cooking gas by toasting the lunchtime sandwiches on my forehead.

At this point, I would like to propose a personal vote of gratitude to Jonas Salk, Howard Florey, and the Alphapharm Pharmaceutical Company. Where would we be without these national Australian treasures? Sure, two of them are American, but that's splitting hairs. Within six hours of taking my first antibiotic, I was already improving.

Twenty-four hours later, I was mostly better. I still had a sore throat, but the weakness and fever were gone. Most of the bacteria were obviously dead, bar a few survivors in my throat.

We humans like to think of ourselves as the top of the food chain and masters of the planet. But nothing could be further from the truth. We've only been here a lazy couple of million years. The real rulers of the known universe are bacteria – they've had the run of the place for about three billion years. We're only here because they're letting us stay, probably so that they can feast on our garbage, and live in our intestines. But one day they're going to sneak under the guard of our pharmaceutical companies, and a drug-resistant bacterium is going to wipe us all out. Every one of us. We are alive only because they have not   figured   out   how   to   do   it.   Yet.

But have you ever seen bacteria growing in a bottle of bourbon? No, you haven't, have you? No mould, no germs, no nothing. You know why? Bacteria hate the stuff. They can't stand it. It burns their little bacterium bodies, and makes them scream little bacterium screams of pain before they die.

As I recovered, I ruminated on how the bacteria in my throat had caused me a lot of pain over the preceding four days. I longed for revenge. *It was payback time.*

I poured myself a triple bourbon, and added a splash of coke for colour. As I threw it down my throat, I could feel those little bastard-bacteria suffering. I could feel them burning. They were in pain, lots of pain. I smiled a cruel, cold smile.

But I didn't stop there, oh no. I poured another triple, but this time drank it slowly. Why burn them with a match, when I could slowly roast the little bastards over hot coals? But I still wasn't satisfied. I had another, and another, then yet another. I reasoned that if I was still standing then they probably were too. Finally, after a long (but fun) afternoon, the bottle was mostly empty. My mission was complete. Revenge had never tasted so *sweet*.

Perhaps I should get back to the holiday. Our time in Kununurra, my illness aside, was pleasant. It was a terrific little town in which to be stuck. It had every basic facility, and because the campground was in the centre of town, we could walk everywhere. That's a big bonus when you don't have a car.

We were also somewhat fortunate that our car broke down right in the middle of the Beijing Olympics. We'd barely seen any television on the trip so far, so we took this as an opportunity to take it easy for a few days. I picked up a brand new TV from the local Target store for $65, and plonked myself in front of it.

Can you believe they can sell a brand new TV for $65 in a place like Kununurra? My business mathematics (I even managed to work this out without Kath's help) tells me that the store would need at least $20 profit to keep functioning, so the distributors must have sold it to them for $45. I am sure that they would also want $20 for their troubles, meaning that Conia, the manufacturer, must have made it for about $15 to leave a profit. Fifteen lousy dollars! You couldn't buy the parts for that.

Despite being out of touch with everything Olympic, it took me all of two hours to grow heartily sick of the name Michael Phelps. How did the rest of the free world cope with this stuff for two weeks? Within a couple of days we realised that TV was not going to be the time-filler that we thought it would be. When you don't have access to a television you barely miss it, but I was surprised to be reminded in such rapid and unequivocal terms of just how much bullshit it contains.

There were, of course, plenty of Olympic highlights. Who could ever forget the sight of Khetag Gazyumov of Azerbaijan, taking home the bronze medal in the Men's 96kg freestyle wrestling competition. Then there was Zuzana Stefecekova winning silver in the women's trap shooting. I'm sure that all Slovakians stood, as I did, and cheered until they were hoarse. And, in scenes that will forever be etched in all our memories, I feel privileged to have witnessed the two gold medals won by Badar-Uugan Enkhbat and Tuvshinbayar Naidan for Mongolia. Two gold medals! Now I know this is a bit disrespectful, but I'm just asking an honest question here: Did anyone else get just a teensy little bit sick of hearing that Mongolian national anthem?

Despite exhausting ourselves watching those classic moments, we managed to extricate ourselves from in front of the box and explore the town. One evening we took an expedition on "The BBQ boat". Kununurra is built along the Ord River, which they have dammed to form Lake Kununurra. A plethora of companies offer all sorts of cruises, but when we heard that there was one that not only showed you the sights, but offered you six types of meat for dinner, it was a no-brainer. I had all six, by the way. Twice each.

We also had two trips to the races. Our timing in this department was impeccable, as Kununurra only has two race days per year, and our little stay overlapped them both. I have always loved country race days, and Kununurra's two-day carnival did not disappoint. It was well organised, fun and convivial. We went the whole shebang – folding chairs, picnic lunch, nibblies, drinks for the kids, and of course, the obligatory hip flask of bourbon.

My betting form was hot. Twice, I just missed picking the trifecta, with my fancies finishing first, second and fourth*. I also bought a horse in a Calcutta auction, and despite getting it at a good price, it was a waste of money. But I fared better than the bloke who bought number five. His fancy broke from the barrier, immediately turned around, and took off through the hills. As far as I know, it's still out there. Literally still running….

The organisers devised a cheap way to keep the ground clear of used betting tickets. They had a kids' draw in which you had to write your name on the back of a used ticket and put it in a barrel. After the last race on each day one ticket was drawn, with the winning kid taking home $50 for his or her troubles.

On the first Saturday's race day, the Perrier offspring pecked the ground like chickens for a couple of hours, picking up discarded tickets. Unfortunately, their efforts were overwhelmed when the used Calcutta raffle tickets were monopolised by another gang of kids. But on the second Saturday, they came prepared. Pens at the ready, they scavenged, begged and cajoled every spare betting slip on course. They had plenty of competition, but stuck at their task doggedly. Strategically, they positioned themselves front and centre at the Calcutta draw, and seized upon the leftover tickets like hungry seagulls onto a chip. They even recruited Kath to do some scribing for them in the tense final hour. The result? Victory to Team Perrier! $50, straight into the kicker.

---

* Ok, I admit there were only four horses in each race.

As a responsible dad, I thought it important to teach my kids a sense of fair play. Like anyone who has experienced an unexpected windfall, they, after some gentle encouragement from me, agreed to buy a celebratory round of drinks. Yes kids, $50 only buys five cans of bourbon and coke. That's why daddy carries a hip flask.

In the middle of our stay at Kununurra, we rented a car and headed out of town. This was partly to explore the surrounding region, but primarily so that we could sit in air conditioning for a few hours.

Our first stop was Keep River National Park, just over the border into the Northern Territory. It was a fine little park. We had a lovely 3 km mid morning walk through the sandstone domes and cliffs. We looked at some aboriginal relics, and sat in a cool tunnel near a mountain top to cool down. It felt nice to be travelling again.

As the heat increased, we needed an excuse to drive further, and so headed about 160 km north east to the town of Wyndham. I'm really pleased we went to Wyndham. Savour those words: "I'm really pleased we went to Wyndham". It's unlikely that you'll ever see them in print again, even if you live to be one hundred.

A friend of mine at home is a top-class real estate agent. I know that, in most people's minds, this immediately qualifies him as a top-class wanker, but please put that issue aside for the moment. He told me that the real art of being successful in real estate is attracting new listings - the houses then simply sell themselves. Were he to migrate this philosophy to Wyndham, he would soon be like everyone else in town: broke. Nearly every house in Wyndham was for sale, and every business premise (bar three) was for lease.

Wyndham is joining the ranks of Casper, Mrs Muir's Captain and Patrick Swayze: it's becoming a ghost. It barely had more life than the decommissioned Wittenoom. It was sad, yet intriguing, to behold.

We experienced a seminal example of this ghost-town persona during a visit to Wyndham's crocodile farm. Long before the legendary Steve Irwin had even collected his first gecko, Wyndham had a crocodile farm. In fact, it was the first croc farm in Australia, and is the landmark tourist attraction in the region. We scheduled our visit to coincide with the advertised 2 pm feeding tour.

We duly arrived at the gate in our rented 4WD at 1.45pm. The car park was empty, but we entered the reception nevertheless. A sign on the wall stated: "The tour has already started. Please enter via the side door and catch up with the group." Sure enough, only 10 metres away was the side door, emblazoned with another sign indicating the entrance.

We wandered through, and, after winding along a café veranda and a connecting walkway, we entered the zoo proper. We traversed a few pathways, but couldn't see anything resembling a tour. Nor could we see any employees. For that matter, we couldn't see a single other person. The only living things we could see were the crocs in the pens, so it was to them that we devoted our attention.

You may recall from Chapter Nine that I dissed freshwater crocodiles for being so wimpy. Well, today we met their big brothers, the salties. Trust me, I wouldn't say a word against these guys. They were monsters. It was really spooky when their eyes followed you as you walk across the path. Nothing moving ... except the eyes....

We kept ambling, looking at crocs – big 'uns, baby 'uns, happy couples, groups, singles. Lots and lots of crocs. But still no people. It's difficult to describe how eerie it felt to be so alone. So after an hour or so we left, without even paying the entrance fee. Great value for money! The drive back through Wyndham was as crowded as the croc zoo.

I feel for Wyndham. Somebody, at some stage, made a genuine effort to present the town well. Many of the buildings are 150 years old, and are thoughtfully signposted to highlight their past. They've built statues to honour the original aboriginal inhabitants, and have the world's biggest fake croc statue. Wyndham's central hill has a spectacular lookout, with a vista that covers the mouths of *five* rivers.

But the town is dead. They could run a dozer through the place and nobody would notice for months. If Wyndham were a fish, it would be floating upside down in the bucket, forlornly flapping its gills.

Eventually we left the eerie empty town, and headed 'home' to Kunna (after a few weeks you qualify as a local and can use the shortened version). The rest of our time at Kunna was spent taking it easy – much like you would on any two or three week camping holiday. We read lots of books, visited some impressive aboriginal art galleries, zipped around the lake on a hired boat, went to the outdoor movie theatre, and drank plenty of beer and wine trying to keep cool.

Like Wyndham, Kununurra also had a great mountain lookout, and like Wyndham's it had an unlikely location: in the centre of town. It was a steep, high hill called *The Knob*. We joined a dozen others – even including a few locals – on the summit to watch the sunset one evening.

We also took a walk through "Celebrity Tree Park" which is situated near the town lake. Whenever a celebrity stayed in town, they were asked to plant a tree, which was subsequently marked with a plaque. Luminaries so far include Princess Anne, singer Johnny Farnham, and actor Bud Tingwell, along with all 800 previous Governors-General of Australia.

We kept a low profile on Jake's 'top try-scorer' award for Easts Tigers Rugby Under 8 Blue, lest they wanted him to plant a tree; it was just too darn hot to bother with legacies. I am sure that if Badar-Uugan Enkhbat and Tuvshinbayar Naidan ever stop through en route from Mongolia, they will hand them a Boab seedling and a garden trowel before they know it. They might even play the Mongolian national anthem while they dig.

Finally, two and a half weeks after our accident, the final parts for our car's repair arrived via donkey-mail.

The mechanic was optimistic that it would take him only another couple of days or so to get everything back together. Suddenly we had much to do. The camp site needed to be cleaned and packed. The park accounts needed to be settled. We had to pick up the car, take it for a test drive and pay the bill. With so many jobs that had to be completed in a short space of time, I did what any sensible man would do: I booked myself onto an all day fishing trip.

As you know, I had long been on a quest to catch a barramundi, thus far to no avail. I had already cast out about a half a dozen times on trip without success. With time running short, and a lot of touring to cram in once we hit the road again, I sensed this was my last chance to catch one of these elusive fish.

The minibus picked me up at 5.45 am (ugh) and we headed along a bush track to a place called "Macca's Barra Camp". After a quick coffee, we hit the water, and by 7.30 am, we (three guests and a guide) were trolling the Ord River for barra.

Barra fishing is a sport of great contrast. For long periods you just sit there, lazily flicking your rod, hoping to lure one of the buggers out from under a log. The conversation idles along, and occasionally stops altogether. The only sounds are the low hum of the boat engine, squawks from the malley geese overhead, and the occasional cawing of crows or galahs. You feel warm and relaxed. Sleepy.

Suddenly, you feel an almighty rip on the end of your line.

"I'm on!" you yell instinctively.

Like clockwork, the guide reacts. He powers up, and jets the boat to the centre of the river, away from the rocks and snags. The other anglers wind in furiously so that their lines don't interfere with your retrieval. And you, well, you wind your reel for all you're worth.

The rod bends to breaking point as you struggle to overpower the barra – it feels like you've snagged a cow on your hook. Then suddenly – whoosh – you see a flash of silver as it leaps out of the water, flexing furiously, in a final attempt to throw your lure.

Over the next minute or two you keep straining – pull up, wind down, pull up, wind down – until you can see the fish flashing its colours at you from beneath the boat. Many catches are lost at this point, so the battle is not over yet. You keep your line tight, and your rod bent. Finally, the guide scoops the fish up with a net, and dumps it, flapping and kicking, onto the floor of the boat. You've landed a barra! You little beauty!

After the lure is removed comes the all important measuring. In WA, you can keep only those fish between 55 cm and 80 cm. Those that are bigger (i.e. breeding females - all large barra are female) or smaller, must be returned to the river. If you are lucky, and your catch measures between these limits, then you have not only landed a fish, but three night's dinner as well.

By the end of the day, I had landed four of these amazing fish. Two of them were keepers, with the biggest being 68cm.

I was darned pleased with myself, but one little part of me nagged that my quest was not fully over. After all, this had been an organised fishing expedition on which any mug who could hold a rod would probably have caught a couple. It felt a little like beating your kids at Monopoly, or perhaps how Olympic athletes feel when they have won a race after taking steroids; it's great to be the champion, but the feeling was just a little hollow. The final part of my challenge remained.

Still, those barra fillets tasted bloody good on the barbeque that night.

Chapter 13: Kununurra again

After three weeks of patient waiting, we were finally on the verge of leaving Kununurra. After a delay of two weeks waiting for a new engine, and then a third week for a new clutch kit, we were bursting to get going. Although Kunna was fine, I doubt that too many people would choose to spend 25% of their entire Australian outback holiday in a small northern WA town. Besides, if we had stayed any longer, they would have tried to include us on the electoral roll.

It was with great relief that we received a telephone call from the mechanic one afternoon. Instead of him conveying one of his usual messages, which was either...

(a) I can't get hold of the parts for (insert random number between five and ten) days,
(b) they've sent me the wrong part,
(c) you'd better come around and look at this John, I've found another serious problem that is going to add thousands of dollars to your repair bill,

... he actually had some good news. The car would be ready *tomorrow*.

In a premature frenzy, Kath began washing, cleaning and packing every scrip and scrap of camping gear. It was like a pregnancy nesting reflex on steroids. She implored, nay demanded, that we help her, and within the hour all our chattels were neatly trussed away in the camper trailer.

The next morning dawned as it had for the previous 19 in Kunna: bright, blue, and searingly hot. Because we had already packed away our chairs, tables, books, shade, and everything else, we had naught to do but sit around and wait for the final telephone call from the mechanic. So we found a park bench and waited. And waited. And waited some more.

Despite the fact that the phone was never more than an arm's reach away, we checked the missed calls and message bank every half an hour, just in case. But the damn telephone just wouldn't ring.

At this stage, I wish to apologise to Jodie Stewart. I met Jodie at a Grade Ten dance at school. We hit it off - I even scored a pash - and I promised to ring her the next day. But I chickened out. I never rang. After enduring that morning in Kununurra, I now know how it feels to sit by the telephone, waiting for a call that never arrives. So Jodie, should you ever be reading this, I'm sorry. You no doubt found someone better anyway.

By midday, the extreme heat had baked my patience to a thin-and-crispy level. I called Pete the mechanic to see how the final stages of repair were progressing.

"Just a few little things to iron out. Won't be long. Don't worry. I'll call you as soon as she's ready."

So we sat, wandered around town, sat around some more, had lunch, and then crammed in a bit more sitting around just after lunch. Our tolerance was almost fully drained when, at about 3pm, the telephone finally rang.

"Hi Pete," I answered excitedly. I knew it was Pete the mechanic because I had given him his own ring tone on my phone.

"Hi John," he replied. "This is just a courtesy call...."

Courtesy call?

... "to let you know that..."

Just tell me the car's ready, Pete.

.... "that unfortunately...."

Don't you dare.

.... "due to unforeseen circumstances...."

No.

.... "your car won't be ready...."

Please.

.... "until tomorrow."

Damn.

I hung up.

"Tomorrow," was all that I had to say to Kath and the kids as we traipsed back to the campsite. Laboriously, unenthusiastically, we unpacked, re-assembled and re-erected our campsite for our 20th night in Kununurra.

We woke up the next morning to discover that our laptop computer had been stolen. It was not only a computer that had been stolen, but also all of our photos, music, movies, and of course, my typed trip notes. Whoever had taken all of this away from us had probably unloaded it for $50. Burn in hell, you mongrel. It was not a good start to the day, but I had no doubts that things would improve.

Yeah, right.

We again re-packed our camp, and then sat around. It was eerily similar to the previous day. Finally, at about midday, we received *the call*. I veritably sprinted down the road, hopping over a couple of fences and ducking through some back yards that I'd discovered made a good short cut. Then I followed the trail through the grass that I had forged over the previous three weeks, arriving at the depot not more than a couple of minutes after the phone first rang. Shortly thereafter, I was finally taking our Jackaroo for a *drive*.

However, we weren't quite out of town yet. The air-conditioning, which is as vital as the steering wheel in this part of the world, wasn't working. Not unless you count blowing 45 degree air into the car as "working".

The mechanic directed us to the local aircon guy, who had apparently re-installed our system after the engine change. He looked at it gravely for a few minutes, then rubbed his chin, and then looked gravely at me again.

"I'll have to take it out the back," he declared.

In my meagre experience of this life so far, being "taken out the back" is either really fun or horribly bad. The aircon guy's expression told me this wasn't the fun kind.

So we sat around in his office for an hour – we were getting very good at this by now – while he did whatever it was he was doing out the back. Probably just having a cigarette. When he returned, he told us that the problem was that the compressor wasn't properly adjusted for the heat (misdiagnosis #1) and that he could fix it. Thank goodness. But then he continued "but I can't fit you in for a couple of days."

Two more nights in Kununurra, or a hot drive out of town? We were on the road before he'd finished his sentence. Or had the chance to give us a bill.

I'm sure you can imagine our relief as we turned and waved our last goodbyes to this little outback town. Finally, finally, finally, we were on the road again. Although our stay was nice enough under the circumstances, we were all very pleased that we were leaving Kununurra forever. Never to return. Ever.

An hour later, we putted into the mechanic's bay in - you guessed it - Kununurra. We'd only made 30km out of town before the engine system warning lights came on, including the one that said "stop driving now, you idiot". They refused to go out, no matter how hard I hit the dashboard.

The last time I had seen that particular light illuminated was when I was in the middle of a certain river crossing at El Questro. The memories of this warning light now haunted me as we sat in Pete the mechanic's shed, awaiting the arrival of "the guy from Holden". I think this referral was Pete's way of saying "I know you've got a potentially serious problem, most likely which was caused through my failure to properly re-install your engine, but now I've got to work on someone else's car for a while." I sensed that "a while", in this case, meant "forever".

So the Perrier family did what we do best: we sat around doing nothing, waiting for a mechanic. Said Holden guy duly arrived, and, after half an hour of poking about with his computer-gizmo-thing and gravely rubbing his chin, he deemed that the engine was OK but the sensor was damaged. Of course, he could fix the sensor if we wanted him to, but it would take him a couple of days to get the….

No thanks. Just give me my keys, mate. We're out of here. (Again, fiendishly departing before any suggestion could be made that we somehow owed them more money.)

And so it was that, at 3 pm, some 30 hours after our original ETD, we permanently departed Kununurra for the second time, with the warm red glow of an engine warning light and an even warmer, non-air-conditioned breeze accompanying us as we drove.

Chapter 14: Katherine

After a night at a roadside stop, we arrived in Katherine. Jacob thought it hilarious that his mum, Katherine, was in Katherine. In fact, he felt so moved by the comedy of this situation that he repeated the joke for the entire 30km from town to the national park.

The park, whose official aboriginal name is Nitmiluk, is more commonly referred to as Katherine Gorge, but please do not tell Jake unless you want a 20-minute monologue on the merriment of Katherine swimming in Katherine Gorge.

After setting up camp, we took a walk to familiarise ourselves with the park. There was a three kilometre loop track around the top edge of the gorge, which seemed an ideal choice. Even though the afternoon was hot, we enthusiastically embarked upon a family hike.

An hour later we emerged from the bush, panting, red-faced, thirsty and exhausted. I'm not sure how many human beings have ever melted or spontaneously combusted, but we were close.

It was hot. Damn hot. I've heard rumours that Hell is a fairly warm sort of place. One day I'll probably get to make a direct comparison, and I'm taking all bets that Katherine that day was hotter. We subsequently discovered that the ground temperature at camp was 45 degrees. The rangers told us that the top of the gorge, which was bare and rocky and exposed to the sun all day, was routinely ten degrees hotter than base camp. By these measurements, we had just walked three kilometres in 55 degree heat!

Let's just say that our subsequent swim in the cool, clear waters of the gorge was welcome – as was the week's worth of beer that I downed that evening to rehydrate myself. Yes, yes, I know. Beer is a diuretic that makes you excrete fluids, blah blah blah. But have you ever tried to drink 12 stubbies of *water*?

The next day was Father's day. Due to the ever-present heat, we decided to stay closer to the water, so we hired a few canoes to paddle up the gorge. It was a mere $35 each, with no discount for kids, even the ones who were too young to paddle effectively i.e. all of them. At $175 for a couple of hours paddling, I expected High Tea when we returned. But no, we were not even offered a glass of water, much less Angel cakes and Earl Grey.

The price irked me. Think of all the fun you could have with $175 in different circumstances. That's four good tickets to the footy, five bottles of bourbon, six good feeds of eye fillet, 17 bets at the races, or about 150 cans of beer – or any reasonable combination of the above. It has to be better than two hours of paddling a canoe up Katherine Gorge, but there was little to do other than put those thoughts aside and get on with our expedition.

The kids paddled admirably for the first hour as we had a relaxed look at the gorge, as well as dumping ourselves over the side for a dip when the going got too hot. But the return journey was a different story. The kids ran out of puff, so we had to rope the canoes together in a train, with myself as the engine at the front. Memories of Rottnest Island flooded back. By the time we got back, the sun and the exertion had me so knackered that I desperately needed a sleep.

Unfortunately, we had pre-booked onto an afternoon boat trip up the gorge. I was simply too tired to stay awake, so I snoozed while we cruised. But I opened my eyes for long enough to take in some of the spectacular scenery of the gorge, with its fortress-like red sandstone walls, and deep cool water. The kids seemed to enjoy the cruise as well, but they unwittingly damned it with faint praise when they agreed the highlight was the unlimited supply of muesli bars.

Just south of Katherine was another feature of the area, the Cutta Cutta caves. We arrived at the caves mid afternoon. Our thermometer indicated 49.5 degrees – a new record - as we set off past the closed visitor's centre on the 600m walk to the cave mouth. Two hours later, we arrived at the cave. Well, it seemed that long anyway; damn, it was hot! A woman in an official-looking khaki uniform sat at the entrance, smoking a cigarette. Every uniform in the NT, whether it is for a postal worker, an army cadet, a pizza delivery boy, or the Anglican bishop, seems to be khaki.

"Did youse buy a ticket?" she inquired of us.

"Ah, no, the visitor's centre was closed."

"That's 'cos I was here," she replied.

I wasn't sure how to respond, so I let her last statement hang.

"So youse wanna tour?"

"No, we came all the way out here just to watch you sit on your fat arse and smoke cigarettes," I replied.

No, I didn't really, but that's what I was thinking. In fact, I politely replied that, yes, we'd love a tour.

"Wiff a guide or without?" she asked.

"Are there guides available?"

"I'm a guide, but I'm a bit busy at the moment.

I looked around. There was nobody about. Obviously she meant "I'm busy smoking my cigarette."

"There's another group that I'm showin' around at the moment," she continued. "They're inside. I'm waitin' for 'em to come out."

Obviously a very personal, detailed tour.

"Youse can go in by yourselves if you want, or youse can wait till I'm finished this tour. It'll probably take about 15 more minutes."

"We'd like a guide if possible," I repeated. "That is, as long as you're not too busy."

She looked a bit annoyed at this choice, but in time she gently nodded and returned to the pressing business of lighting another cigarette. Five minutes elapsed but still there was no sign of the other group's return. The khaki woman then spoke up.

"Youse won't need a torch or nuffin'. The path's lit, and the good bits is lit up even more."

She was clearly trying to fob us off, making it obvious that she did not want to go into that cave *again*. But again we politely declined her offer to go ahead without her. If it were only 10 more minutes, we would rather wait and have some "expert" commentary. After another few minutes' silence, she piped up again.

"Youse can go in for nuffin' if you go now. If youse wait for me, I'm gunna have to charge youse full price."

I doubted that this arrangement was certified as standard practice by the National Parks and Wildlife Authority. However, we were bound by the Cheapskate Travellers Code of Conduct, meaning we were obliged to accept the freebie. So we accepted this final offer from the country's laziest tour guide, and entered the cave – guideless and torchless, but about $40 better off in pocket.

The Cutta Cutta caves tour proved excellent value for money. As promised, the path throughout was sensibly illuminated by LEDs on the guide rails, with spotlights on the interesting features. The 600m journey to the cave's end was punctuated by some impressive cone shaped things that hung down from the ceiling or poked up from the floor, some big shiny glittering rocks, and some wavy shaped things.

Had the guide got off her lazy butt and accompanied us on this burdensome walk, she might have explained that these were in fact stalactites, stalagmites, quartzite formations and cathedral-vaned limestone deposits. At least that's what my best recollections of Grade Ten science told me they were.

Nevertheless, the expedition was well worthwhile. Visually it was spectacular, and, what's more, it was cool. When we returned to the entrance, the guide was exactly as we had left her, except that her cigarette packet was no doubt lighter by about half a dozen sticks.

"That was excellent," we all commented as we filed past her.

She smiled weakly, and then replied unenthusiastically "Yer, it's great, innit?"

"By the way," I added as we headed on the return walk to the car park, "The group you sent down before us ... we didn't see them anywhere."

"Oh bugger," she replied, suddenly agitated. "I told them to stick to the main tunnel. Now I'm gunna have to go in and look for 'em."

I flashed her a sarcastic grin, which was meant to convey "Serves you right, you lazy cow" in the nicest possible way. We then marched our way through the wall of heat back to our even hotter vehicle and were on our way.

The car air conditioner still wasn't working. The dash warning light was still staring at me, like an evil eye, as we drove north. Nevertheless our car was *going*, so we took advantage of this rare situation and headed to Litchfield National Park.

If you talk to most people about top-end national parks in Australia, Kakadu is the often place that springs first into the conversation. For the life of me I can't figure out why, for its western neighbour, Litchfield, is a delight in every way, while for me Kakadu can be as boring as the poo of its own bats. As the locals say, Litchfield-do, Kaka-don't.

Litchfield is Mother Nature's version of an amusement park. In every corner waits a little themed arcade: Termite Alley, the Lost City, the Water Parks, and the Adventure Trail (my terms, by the way). You can't help but have fun.

Our first stop was Termite Alley. The insects up here obviously use the same air-conditioning guy that we used in Kununurra, and hence have devised other ways of keeping themselves cool. Two solutions have emerged, both of which create a dramatic landscape. One species of termite has evolved mounds that are tall, thin slabs, oriented in a north-south direction. The slabs can be over six feet high, yet rarely exceed 20 cm thick. In the afternoon, when the sun is at its hottest, all the termites inside migrate to the shaded eastern face of the mound, keeping a few degrees cooler.

The other species of termite builds very tall mounds with vanes and buttresses that catch the breeze and provide shade. These spires can be up to a massive seven metres tall. Their size and shape has earned them the moniker "Cathedral mounds". We passed by about 250 of these Cathedral mounds, which I think, according to strict Christian doctrine, accumulated enough credit points to excuse me from church for five years.

After wandering around Termite alley for a while, it was time to go to Litchfield's main attraction: the Water Park. It boasted half a dozen swimming areas, each with their own style and character. Our favourite was Buley's Rockholes, a series of family-sized pools, with tumbling little waterfalls and cascading streams bubbling at their entrances and exits.

Buley's also housed some unusual fauna in loose captivity. I believe their scientific name is *Europus Backpackerus*. They tended to congregate in small groups, and had evolved to handle the local extreme heat by shedding most of their clothing. I found that the female of the species was particularly spectacular viewing, and I'm pretty sure that Kath cast some furtive yet admiring glances at the male specimens on display as well.

The Water Park had other rides and attractions, including three spectacular waterfalls, a couple of swimmable creeks, and the lovely Wangi Falls. Wangi is a large waterhole, by my guess about 50 metres in diameter. Two tall waterfalls, side by side, cascade down the high cliffs at the far end. The whole area is surrounded by rainforest, through which you can wander if you somehow tire of the cool, clean water. We camped alongside Wangi, and subsequently swam and lazed about in it for about four hours per day. It was just gorgeous.

In between swims, we visited the Lost City. This corner of the theme park consists of an acre or two of bizarrely shaped rocks. The landscape looked like the remnants of an ancient alien civilisation, whose inhabitants had been killed by beetles that ate their stomachs from the inside out, and then devoured their bones, and everything else, so that there was no trace of the alien beings except the buildings. At least that is what I told the kids on the way there. They said they didn't believe me, but I noticed that they were unusually vigilant in applying the insect repellent before leaving the car.

The Lost City also formed the world's premier venue for kids' climbing and exploring – plastic adventure playgrounds can only dream of this grandeur. If there were ever a world championship in Hide-and-go-seek, then the Lost City at Litchfield would be the perfect venue. So that's what we did: for an hour, we climbed, jumped and then played hide-and-go-seek with the kids. Simple pleasures, simple fun. They loved it.

I defeated the kids at Hide-and-go-seek, too. Only cheated twice.

We also took a drive along the 'Adventure Trail' section of Litchfield Amusement Park. The centrepiece was the ruin of an old tin mine. The mine shaft had fence across it, adorned with a large, clear sign that read "Danger. Do not enter. The shaft may collapse. Admission strictly prohibited."

Inside the mine shaft was very dark and spooky. It also smelled of bat shit. But at least it was cool. If I had a torch, I could have gone further than a lousy ten metres - at least far enough so that I couldn't hear

Kath yelling at me to get out of there. Don't you just love "No entry" signs?

We were en route to another section of the adventure trail, housing a waterfall and the ruins of the old homestead, when we encountered a creek crossing. With our disaster at El Questro still haunting us, we voted five-nil to abandon this section of our expedition in favour of an ice cream at the kiosk.

OK, call me chicken if you must, but later that night the ranger told us they'd just towed a 4WD out of that same creek crossing. Silly bastard had sucked in some water and blown his engine. Really, they should keep these green, gung-ho drivers out of the national parks.

Our final morning at Litchfield was September 11th. The rest of the world may remember a particularly nasty series of plane crashes that happened on this day, but our family prefers to commemorate the birth of our second child, Lachie. He turned nine that day in Litchfield, and was thoroughly delighted with his present of a didgeridoo. He quickly put his spare air to good use.

Chapter 15: Darwin

When holidaying, many people have a theme for their travels. Some people visit museums or national parks. Others hop from one golf course to the next, while other eminently more sensible travellers stagger from one outback pub to another. The Perrier family's theme? Motor mechanics.

After packing up at Litchfield, we headed north to Darwin. In keeping with our tour theme, we headed straight for the local mechanic, where we had booked in for a repair of the air-conditioner and the engine sensor.

Because we would again be without a vehicle, we opted to stay in a hotel near the Darwin central business district (read: pub and restaurant precinct) in preference to camping. Kath selected a small establishment on the edge of town called ... well, for reasons that will soon become obvious I won't tell you what it was called. I can only give you a hint that it was named after a famous Territorian fish species. We booked in advance for three nights. After two months of campervanning, we were looking forward to little taste of civilisation. A hotel room would be a splendid change.

"Hmmm," was my first thought as we entered reception. This opinion was, as it turned out, my most generous assessment of the place. As we looked around, it was clear that the "lodge" was not quite what Kath had in mind when she had booked – and I quote – "a self-contained, two-bedroom, five-bed apartment with a kitchen."

It is fair to compare this hotel to a large crater dug into the ground and filled with excrement, for it truly was a shit hole.

For a start, our "apartment" had only one room. (Sigh … the Campervan Kama Sutra manual would have to be called upon again.) The windows were adorned by scrappy curtains that overhung louvres – some metal, some glass, some absent – which in any event were uncloseable. An old box-style air-conditioner unit rattled away in the corner, barely managing the keep the room below boiling point. Into this room was crammed a lumpy double mattress, and a set of small bunks. The fifth bed? Someone procured a greasy vinyl mattress from a storeroom.

The owners obviously defined "kitchen" differently to most people; they thought it meant "a portable hotplate, a saucepan and a kettle". The fridge was no bigger than an esky, and had six inches of frosting around the ice cube tray. Ick.

I am not normally fussy on such matters, but the crockery was completely mismatched, with the drink receptacles represented by a tin mug, a coke glass that was once available free from Pizza Hut, and a chipped china teacup that somebody's grandma had bequeathed. It was a similar jarring mismatch with the plates and cutlery.

The worst of the horrors was the ablutions block. There was only one shared external toilet for the entire floor. Ditto the shower, whose door would not latch closed. The whole toilet area had the same lovely non-closing louvres as our room. And possibly a peephole camera in the ceiling.

The external toilet arrangement presented an extra problem. When bush camping, if you need to have a pee at night you only need to stumble a couple of metres from the tent. Whatever you were wearing at the time, however much or little, was fine. But at "The Lodge", you had to hike down an external hall, meaning that you had to get dressed to relieve yourself.

Pulling on a pair of shorts at midnight doesn't sound too difficult, does it? But when you are sharing a single bedroom with four other people, the sound of one person fumbling in the dark to firstly locate and then don some clothes usually rouses someone else. They, of course, then decide to go for a pee as well, in the process waking someone else while dressing. So before long we were having a midnight family game of dress-ups, before parading down to the toilet block in turn.

The other guests – I guess you could call them guests, but only by stretching the meaning of the term – were a kids' basketball squad from WA. There were dozens of the little buggers, perpetually emerging like vermin from every nook and cranny. At night they were worse. The yakking and yabbering and background noise were incessant. At this point, I'd also like to apologise to my Mum and Dad for bouncing the basketball in the house when I was fifteen. I now realise just how bloody annoying that sound can be.

All this *luxury* for only $120 per night. Give me camping any day.

The only redeeming feature of "The Lodge" was that Kath was responsible for booking it, not me, so I could give her stick about it for three days. She was clearly tired of the jibes after the first ten minutes, but I persisted nevertheless. Yes, I was childish and immature, but it made me feel better, OK?

Despite the un-luxurious nature of our lodgings, we optimistically set out to explore Darwin. My mate AJ had been married in Darwin a decade previously, and a few of the lads and I had trekked north to help him celebrate. It was a brilliant week, and I had such fond memories of Darwin that I wanted to recreate for my family the best parts of that previous visit.

For some reason, Kath and the kids whinged and whined about this plan after the first stop, and never got into the spirit of the whole adventure. What was wrong, I ask you, with a bit of pre-lunch entertainment at the Parap Hotel strip club?

Instead, we embarked upon the humble tourist route. Because the car was yet again being repaired we were on foot, and the ever-present heat limited us to a few blocks. But this range was within reach of the city centre, where Lachie chose the Hog's Breath Café as the venue for his birthday lunch. My steak sandwich was surprisingly good – excellent in fact. But the best was yet to come.

While Lachie was visiting the toilet, Kath secretly ordered him the largest sundae on the menu. When the staff showed up with a bucket-sized goblet filled with ice-cream, cake, berries, waffles, biscuits, topping and whipped cream, all adorned with nine birthday sparklers – well, Lachie's smile lit up the entire Territory north of the tropic of Capricorn. It was a magic moment.

However, we weren't content to stop with a mere standard-issue dessert, even if it was the largest one available in this spiral arm of the Milky Way galaxy. The kids' meals had all been packaged with a free dessert, which turned out to be three scoops of ice cream and topping. Into the goblet/bucket they went, until the concoction was literally bigger than Lachie's head. Caitlin reliably informed me that it contained, among the other ingredients, 25 scoops of ice cream. Yes, she counted them.

We all pitched in to help Lachie eat it. It was a struggle, but after about 30 minutes of unmitigated gluttony, we registered a victory with an empty bowl. We then wobbled to the nearby movie theatre to watch *Dark Knight*, allowing our respective digestive systems valuable rest time in which to each process 5000 calories.

We emerged from the theatre to take a telephone call informing us that the car had been repaired, and was ready for pick up. Hang on, I thought, we only dropped it off this morning. At first I thought it was a gag, but the guy insisted the car was ready to go. Cautiously, in case there were candid cameras on me, I arrived at the mechanic to find that he was telling the truth. The sensor had been replaced, meaning that that evil, insidious warning light would no longer attempt to hypnotise me as we drove. The air-conditioning compressor had also been repaired - apparently, the previous guy had omitted a bolt when he screwed it back together. (Misdiagnosis #2)

That evening, we visited Darwin's famous Mindel Beach Sunset markets. Normally if I had to choose between walking through a crowded market place and eating my own left arm, I would say "pass the sauce". But these markets were surprisingly agreeable.

The setting was in a long park that ran atop the beach dunes, so the air was open and fresh. The sun was setting across the water, and the park hummed with music, the competing voices of hawkers, and the hubbub of the crowd. It was vibrant and interesting.

The market was packed with eclectic food stalls, ranging from Thai, Japanese, Indonesian and Indian food, to Milk Bars selling coconut smoothies. We tried ever so hard to get excited about dinner, but the lunchtime birthday sundae was only half way down our respective alimentary canals, and we still could not fit in another morsel. Instead, we listened to the buskers, including some very dynamic didgeridoo playing, and soaked up the sights. The kids had a turn on a bungee trampoline, which capped off a wonderful birthday for Lachie.

The next day we drove to the Darwin Museum. You may have noticed the absence of museum trips in our travels thus far, as we collectively find them as dull as mathematics classes at school. (Except for Kath, who finds Mathematics classes stimulating and exciting.) However, 20 years previously I had attended an exhibition of a massive storm called Cyclone Tracey and the havoc it had rained upon Darwin. It left an indelible impression on my young mind, and I was keen to see if it was as I remembered, and for the kids and Kath to experience it as well.

It didn't disappoint. The exhibition was stark and graphic. The kids were spellbound as they soaked in just how much carnage that cyclone caused. In the early 1970s Darwin was a small but growing city of about 40 000 permanent residents. Most of them lived in basic fibro-and-corrugated-iron houses. In a mere couple of hours on Christmas Eve 1974, Tracey changed all that.

The photographs and films told the story vividly. This storm didn't just swipe away a roof here and there, or knock down a garden shed. She utterly decimated almost every building in town; in some suburbs, 97% of dwellings were completely destroyed. In most cases, the only structures left standing were the house posts. Around each of these posts, the fierce winds had folded dozens of corrugated iron sheets as though they were cardboard.

One graphic depiction of Tracey's power was inside a sound booth. A clergyman at the time had recorded the noise of the cyclone as it raged outside, which was replayed as you stood in darkness. The warning sign outside the booth that it "may disturb some listeners" was not an idle threat – the kids were genuinely frightened.

To imagine the sound of Cyclone Tracey, first hide yourself under a desk in a completely dark room – on Christmas Eve if you want a truly authentic experience. Crank up the sound of a fierce, howling gale, so strong that it whips the very words from your mouth. Next – and most importantly - imagine the sound of that wind scraping a sheet of corrugated iron along the road at 200 km/h. *Multiply that sound by one thousand.*

Now pretend that a violent, angry mob are attacking your house with planks of wood, and shattering your windows with rocks. Every minute or two have a neighbour pick up his house with a crane and drop it to earth with a thunderous clatter. If you can imagine all of these sounds at once, you will go close to experiencing 24 December 1974, in Darwin. Oh, it would help if your life were in mortal danger. Then you could probably hear your own heart beating as well.

As you can deduce, the Cyclone Tracey exhibit lived up to my distant memories. After that experience, we set off to explore the rest of the museum, which also proved very worthwhile. They had a display of Indigenous Art Award entries, most of which were very appealing. The exception was the picture that won the $25 000 first prize, which, in my humble opinion, was utter dross. It is tempting to imagine the artist, having dropped his paints onto the floor and cleaned the mess up with a cloth, then framing the pigment-stained rag before submitting it to the jury. In what was no doubt a severe case of *the emperor's new clothes*, the judges awarded this muddle the first prize lest they have to reveal that they could not understand its cultural significance.

The museum was also home to a stuffed carcass of 'Sweetheart', a massive crocodile who had terrorised fishermen near Darwin in the 1970s by overturning their boats. Sweetheart had been captured with a view to relocating him, but he drowned during the attempt. His preserved hide has been scaring the bejesus out of museum patrons ever since.

To complete our museum visit we inspected an intelligent display of the Northern Territory's aquatic and animal life. It was an excellent attraction that was well worth the $0.00 entry fee.

After the museum, we wandered down the road to explore the old Fannie Bay Gaol. The gaol had been constructed in the mid 1800s, and operated up until 1960. They even built gallows to hang two immigrants in the 1950s for murdering a taxi driver. The whole story, which has gone down in Darwin infamy, was illustrated through a series of posters and old newspaper clippings.

The historical society also had pages from the old warden's log on display. It listed each prisoner's name, his crime, and his sentence. One listing was for an unfortunate chap named Neil Madsen. Poor old Neil was incarcerated alongside murderers and rapists for two weeks for the heinous crime of ... drunkenness. Thank goodness times have changed or they'd have to recommission a few hundred disbanded jails to cope with all the inmates. Still, if you were locked up, at least you'd have good company.

We left the gaol (which, incidentally, also had free admission) and wandered over the road to the Darwin Trailer Boat Club. This club was an excellent place to have a drink and watch the sun set over the ocean. We duly obliged, and stayed on for a swim, dinner, some more drinks, a kid's movie, and then lingered over a few final drinks to watch the football later that night. It was a fine way to cap off a top day in Darwin.

The next day we awoke, still keen to explore the cream of Darwin's tourist attractions. We had somehow come into possession of a brochure for a place called "Aquascene", which stated that it was "consistently rated as the best tourist attraction in Darwin". I wish they had included an addendum such as "by the owners", for there is no way that anyone without a vested interest would vote this place as the best *anything*. Except, perhaps, for "the best waste of money on the planet".

At the venerated Aquascene, we paid $8 each for the privilege of chucking crusts of stale bread to some ugly mullet in the harbour. Period.

Please, take this advice: if you ever go to Darwin, do not waste one second of your precious life, nor one cent of your hard-earned pay, at Aquascene. Better to buy a $3.00 loaf of bread, and sit solo on the jetty feeding the fish in peace and quiet, rather than jostling with two-dozen other ripped-off tourists.

Despite the patheticness of Aquascene, it inflamed the fishing bug from somewhere deep in my hunter-psyche. So Lachie and I booked a half-day fishing trip in Darwin harbour. Despite another dozen or so patrons on the boat, Lachie and I caught two-thirds of the day's haul. To put it more precisely, I caught two fish, Lachie none, and one other young girl the third. She obligingly donated her fish to the Perrier Family dinner fund, while the other disappointed patrons headed to the fishmongers.

Our final task before leaving Darwin the next morning was to stock up on provisions for our upcoming journey through Kakadu to the Red Centre. We were in a shopping centre car park, packing the last of the groceries into the camp fridge, when Kath piped up.

"John, what's that green stuff at the front of the car?" she asked.

"Green stuff?"

"Yeah, like green watery slime. It seems to be coming from the engine."

Oh dear. A casual inspection showed that the radiator was leaking openly, with the green coolant running freely down the gutter.

A quick call to our trip sponsors - the Royal Automobile Club of Queensland's roadside breakdown service - had the car towed back to our original mechanic. Unfortunately, it was Sunday, which meant at least another two days in Darwin. I trudged back through the heat towards "The Lodge". Of all the places I did not want to be stuck, this poo-hole was it. Luckily, the travel gods smiled on us just this once, for "The Lodge" was apparently booked out.

Ordinarily I would have found this to be a great aggravation, but in this case my irritability was soothed by the thoughts that the next place would not, could not, be worse. Despite the initial inconvenience of having to find another place – on foot, under the blisteringly hot sun - my effort was rewarded. I eventually chanced upon another block of units. These apartments had two bedrooms each – count them, one, two – and a separate living/dining area. They had real kitchens, matching crockery, windows that closed, and three split-system air conditioners.

Best of all, this unit had its *own toilet and bathroom*. The ramifications were staggering. We could now pee at night without dressing or encountering wildlife. We could leave our toothbrushes and toothpaste in mess beside the sink, or drop our dirty clothes on the bathroom floor. It was just like home!

We were beside ourselves with joy. For the rest of the day we did naught but revel in our cosmopolitan setting, watch in-house movies and drink beer. I am not sure how many beers Kath drank, but, judging by the number of empty stubbies on the floor the next morning, I would say it was quite a few.

The next day the mechanic somehow procured the only Jackaroo radiator north of Hobart – big city life has its plusses - and 24 hours later we departed Darwin. The delay had altered our plans, again. After being waylaid in Kununurra for three weeks, we had omitted north Queensland from our itinerary. The two-day delay in Darwin now meant that we had no time for Kakadu, which became Kakadidn't.

But at least we still had time to see Uluru and the Red Centre. Surely, nothing else could go wrong with the car. We motored enthusiastically down the highway, with the new radiator cooling the engine, and our recently repaired air conditioner doing the same to us.

*

The air conditioner lasted an hour. After that, it blew 38-degree air into our 37-degree car. For good measure the stereo died, depriving me of the opportunity to annoy the family with my atrocious singing. We made it back to Katherine, where a helpful auto-electrician named Niall interrupted his lunch break to help us. His diagnosis: the air conditioning compressor was dead. Irretrievably. He uninstalled it so that it would not cause any further problems. We would no longer have air-conditioning, but thankfully we still owned a driveable car. We'd heard worse news, and at least we still had time to make it to Uluru.

Niall installed a new stereo for us and we headed south once again, with me blaring out ABBA hits like "Mamma Mia" and "Waterloo" at full voice. I know, I know, it's very camp, but please grant me one guilty pleasure.

An hour later, we pulled up at the one-pub town of Mataranka. Two screeching, scrangling sounds – one from under the bonnet, and another disharmonious clanking from the rear wheel - informed me that our confidence regrading Uluru was misplaced. Our tour theme of mechanic-hopping was set to strike again.

Mataranka is a tiny outpost on the Stuart Highway in between somewhere and nowhere. It has six buildings – a garage/diner, a general store, a pub, a supermarket, a post office and – for this I will one day individually thank all of the gods – a mechanic. A fine bloke he was too, old Willie. We got to know him very well over the next week as we waited for a fan belt to arrive from Adelaide (2600 km away) and a set of wheel bearings to arrive from Melbourne (3300 km away). So it was that a petrol stop in Mataranka took eight days.

The stopover gave us a chance to renew our acquaintance with Niall the auto-electrician from Katherine, who drove a mere 200km for a service call to install a new air-conditioning compressor. As per the standard *modus operandi* in the outback, he discovered that they sent him the wrong part so he drove back home, re-ordered the new part, paid $120 for a high-speed courier, and returned three days later to install it.

Little by little we explored the town and its surrounds, and by the end of the week we developed a genuine affection for the place. On our second morning, I was chatting with the supermarket checkout lady. After some small talk, I enquired as to what had tempted her to live in a tiny remote town like Mataranka.

"Barramundi," she replied without hesitation.

Since my fishing adventure in Kununurra, I had been eager to renew my acquaintance with barra, so I listened with interest.

"When I caught my first barra here, I was hooked," she said. "I vowed not to leave until I had caught a one metre fish."

"How long have you been here?" I asked.

"Four years."

She must have spotted my ever-so-slightly raised eyebrows, because she quickly added "but I caught one that measured 91 cm last year, so I'm getting close."

"Any local spots you can recommend?" I asked hopefully. The delay in her answer told me that even though she mentioned a few spots, I was not getting the whole truth. Nevertheless, I thanked her for the tips, wished her luck in catching a one-metre barra sooner than 2019, and departed.

I decided to try my hand in the local river that afternoon. Sure, I had caught four barra in Kununurra, but they were on an organised fishing safari. It felt a little bit like cheating. But if I could land one of these grand fish for myself, just from the riverbank – well, that would be something worth writing about. Literally.

I made a few enquiries around the campground. One bloke had been trolling up and down the river for six days without a strike. The park owner had also been trying for a while, but thus far without luck. The consensus was that the fish were "off the boil" at the moment. Despite the dire predictions, I was determined to give it a go. The car's diagnosis, along with the knowledge that we now had no time to visit Uluru, had dampened my spirits. A long tussle with a big fish was called for.

Accompanied by Caitlin, my nominal good luck charm for the day, we headed out of town about 5km to a secluded part of the river. With a low countenance, I picked a lure out of the tackle box, clipped it on, and half-heartedly began casting and retrieving. I sank into a monotonous rhythm:

Cast-flick-wind-flick-wind-flick …
cast-flick-wind-flick-wind-flick …
cast-flick-wind-flick-wind-flick …
cast-flick-wind-flick-wind-flick …
cast-flick-wind-flick-wind-BANG!

Suddenly, I jolted to life. There was a tug on the end of my line. Was it a barra? Then – whoosh – out of the water leapt a shining, writhing, bountiful-looking fish. Caitlin jumped around hysterically and screamed excitedly, performing her role to perfection. I reeled the fish in, laughing ecstatically. I landed a 55cm barra – by myself – on only my fifth cast! You little ripper.

Ten minutes later, I was back at it. Cast, retrieve. Cast, retrieve. After my early success, I felt as though I was doing something right. The combination of lure, line, casting and location had worked once – so it might just work again. If one barra had fallen for my lure, then maybe there were others….

Whack! A huge hit. Then, an irresistible surge on the end of the line. As a giant silver flash exploded from the river fully six feet out of the water, I knew I had a fight on my hands. The line was spooling off the reel – this girl was much bigger than the last. I barely had the strength to pull up the rod tip much less reel in the line. But little by little, leverage won out. I steadily hauled the fish in, kicking and leaping all the way to the bank. When I had finally landed it, I had a 75 cm bundle of barra in my hands. Yeehah.

It took me 15 minutes to retrieve my lure and bleed the fish. I was sweating, hot, and physically buggered. I suggested to Caitlin that, with two big fish already in our keeping, perhaps we should go home.

"Can't we stay fishing for longer daddy?" she pleaded.

Yes, that's right, my daughter was actually pleading with me to stay out fishing. I'm glad I agreed. Five minutes later, I reeled in the biggest fish I had ever laid my eyes on.

The catch itself was exhilarating, much like the fight with the baby 75 cm specimen I had reeled in minutes earlier. But this catch had an added twist: just as I beached it on to the riverbank, the line snapped. All that remained between me and the loss of my best ever fish was a few feet of sandy riverbank.

The fish ferociously tried to flap its way to freedom. What could I do? I had no net. I tried to pick it up by its mouth – the time tested way of holding a barra - but the lure was still inside, with three sharp hooks flapping about, making it too difficult and dangerous. And those razor sharp barra gills looked menacing whenever I tried to grab its body. As it flipped ever nearer the river's edge, I desperately tried to quell it by holding it under my foot. But this fish was just too strong, and with another mighty surge it flapped down to the river, just centimetres from the water's edge. Was I about to lose the greatest catch of my life?

Bereft of other ideas, I flicked it with my foot into a shallow wash out, a small dry gutter. Then I dove onto the fish like a rodeo cowboy tackling a calf. I lay there, effectively pinning this behemoth with my entire body weight.

Now with a milli-moment in which to think, I yelled frantically at Caity to fetch the pliers from the fishing kit. While she ran 50 metres back along the bank toward our fishing gear, I simply lay on the fish, feeling like an amateur Olympic wrestler as I resisted its powerful surges. My face was rubbing into the sandy dirt of the riverbank, I was sweating profusely, and continually wary of being cut by the fish's sharp gills. But I was determined that this epic fight would not result merely in a tale of the one that got away.

Minutes later, Caity arrived back, frantically waving the pliers. I wrested the lure from the barra's mouth,

196

and then firmly gripped inside its jaws, with my other hand under its belly. As all barra do when held this way, it instantly went to sleep. Finally, I had succeeded; although it had taken me ten full minutes, I had landed the best fish of my life.

I carried it back to the car, pausing several times to rest my aching arms. With great anticipation, I stretched my battered tape measure over the length of the fish. In a detail that will forever annoy the lady behind the counter at Mataranka supermarket, this fish measured in at ... wait for it ....101 cm.

Yes, I entered the fabled, rarefied air of the Barramundi Metre Club – on my very first afternoon fishing at Mataranka.

There is a saying out here that if the fish fits in your esky it's too small. I have another version: if the fish won't fit in your car boot, it's bloody big. Fair dinkum, I just couldn't make this barra fit in the back of the Jackaroo. I had to close the hatch over her tail. Now *that's* a sign that you've had a good day's fishing.

When I returned to camp, the faces of Kath and the boys as we presented our catch were priceless. As I pulled those fish from the boot, their faces just exploded in awe and delight. I even detected a hint of admiration in Kath's gaze.

Then she ruined it all by adding: "Gee, John, you were really lucky today, weren't you?"

Pardon? Lucky? You can't be serious. Your hunter-husband has just stalked, caught and killed his prey, returning with dinner for a week, and you tell him he was lucky? Why thanks darling. You look so beautiful when you are wearing makeup.

I had an insatiable urge to share the news of my catch, so I rang my mate Tod - who had joined me on our (unsuccessful) barra fishing trip earlier in the year - on his mobile. I told him about my haul, and excitedly informed him that I had joined the Barramundi Metre Club. But Tod seemed strangely unimpressed. He mumbled something about it being good news, and then bade me goodbye.

I was taken aback. Surely, Tod should have rejoiced in my triumph. He knew more keenly than anyone did how many fruitless hours I had already spent in pursuit of such a trophy catch. Why wasn't he celebrating with more vigour and enthusiasm?

Sure, he was in the USA on business, and I had woken him with this news at 3am. However, if the guy did not want me to keep him in the loop regarding my fishing exploits then he should have turned his bloody mobile off.

Nevertheless, I enjoyed growing attention from other campers as word of the catch filtered through the park. The steady trickle of visitors to our tent site over the next few hours to view the haul stoked my ego to never-before scaled heights. I had a wonderful afternoon, as I slowly cleaned and filleted the fish, had a cold beer or two, and discussed successful combinations of lures, rigging and line choice with other anglers.

This fishing experience had led me to develop a policy that will save the world billions of dollars. Get rid of all the anti-depressant medication. Shed the shelves of mood altering substances, and sack the psychiatrists. For it is impossible to be in a bad mood of any sort for at least a week after a catch like this. So let's get all of our mental health patients to the rivers, lakes and oceans, with rod and reel in hand. I'll volunteer to guide them.

The rest of the week in Mataranka dawdled by at a lovely leisurely pace. Although the car needed major repairs before we could leave town, it was driveable over short distances, meaning we were free to explore. Mataranka has some great swimming holes: Bitter springs, a lovely freshwater billabong; the Mataranka thermal pools; and some natural rock pools and pontoons in the nearby Roper River. We visited at least one of these swimming holes every day.

Mataranka is the heart of "*We of the Never Never*" country, as depicted in the eponymous book and film. The original biopic, written by Mrs Aeneas Gunn, illustrated the life of pioneering Australian families, and gave insight into their relationships with the local indigenous people and the harsh conditions of country life. The Mataranka homestead had a replica of the original settler's home, which was a simple and effective way of bringing the story to life.

The Mataranka pub showed the film every day at noon. Because this historical picture was so important for the children's education, Kath and I surrendered an afternoon to sit in the pub, patiently waiting, while knowledge filled their precious little minds. Ah, the sacrifices we parents make for our children's education.

We discovered another shop in Mataranka that pleased me greatly. I'll tell you why. Twenty years ago, when, as a young tearaway, I hitchhiked my way around Australia, I chanced upon a shop in Alice Springs that sold the most magnificent meat pies. These pies were simply divine, and were so far superior to any other of their ilk that I had eaten before, or since, that they deserved their own separate food group classification.

On our current trip, we had been heading for the Red Centre. Ostensibly, this was to see Uluru and to explore the natural wonders of our country's red heart, but really it was so that I could find that pie shop again. So it was a major blow to my stomach's gastronomical ambitions when our car troubles extinguished that opportunity.

The swings and roundabouts of travel were beautifully epitomised when we walked into the greasy diner at Mataranka for lunch one day. There, proudly sitting in the bain-marie, were the five biggest, fattest, juiciest meat pies I had seen in two decades. And their taste was as impressive as their size. By the time I had devoured two of them, missing Uluru no longer seemed like a big deal. After all, it's only a bloody rock.

After lunch, I ducked in next door to grab some beer to restock my rapidly diminishing supply. After settling upon a carton of beer - it was hot, OK? - I proceeded to the checkout.

"Could I see some ID please," said the straight-faced woman behind the counter.

I paused, checking for a hint of a smile concealed within her tired, taciturn features. No one had asked me for ID since I was 17 years old. Surely, my greying hair, drooping jowls, and middle-aged paunch more than adequately denoted me as being well and truly past the legal drinking age of eighteen.

"Are you trying to pay me a compliment?" I asked, sending her my most boyish, charming smile. She looked at me without a hint of change in her expression, and simply replied "No ID, no service."

At this reply, two thoughts struck me. First, that my boyish charm was not as effective as it once was, and second: what sort of a liquor store would demand identification from someone who was clearly on the latter side of forty years old? However, I wanted the beer more than I wanted to make my point, so I extracted my licence from deep within a long forgotten crevice of my wallet and handed it over.

She studied it as if she was a guard on Checkpoint Charlie during the Cold War. After spending what I thought was far too long assuring herself of its authenticity, she typed my licence number into a computer. After subsequently scrolling though a few screens of data, she eventually, reluctantly, agreed to sell me some beer.

I left the store feeling indignant, and more than a little besmirched. It was as though this woman was checking through my life's history, and making sure that I had been a good little boy, before she would permit me to purchase alcohol. Silly me, for thinking that such a purchase was my right, as an adult Australian. Although I did not know it at the time, my initial guess was far closer to the truth than I imagined.

I soon learned that Mataranka fell under the auspices of the recently introduced Northern Territory National Emergency Response. This law was aimed at reducing alcohol-related violence and other such crimes, with particular emphasis on Aboriginal communities. Along with an increased police presence, firm restriction on alcohol sales was part of the strategy – hence the scrutiny of my driver's licence. I imagine that had I tried to purchase another carton of beer the following day, the system, and the grumpy-faced woman, would have refused me.

Although both sides of parliament had supported the law, some civil libertarians, academics and indigenous leaders condemned it as being an attack on personal freedom, overtly paternalistic, and yet *another* nanny-state initiative, designed to woo voters who were easily seduced by tough talk against crime. Remote and indigenous Australia already had bans on cigarette sales, limits on the sale of various types of alcohol (for example, flagons of fortified spirits), bans on pictures of nudey women, and dozens of other proscribed behaviours. I was not sure which side of the political debate I supported, but as I walked out of that bottle shop, I felt a sense of irritation, and righteous anger, at having my drinking history so clearly laid bare for a complete stranger to inspect. No wonder some of the aboriginal communities felt disrespected and aggrieved by this intervention.

That night, when bedding down in the camp ground, and wondering which one of the 101 campervan Kama Sutra positions I was going to attempt that evening, my coltish enthusiasm was curdled by a spine-chilling scream that echoed across our campsite. The screech, clearly a woman's voice, left no doubt that she was in grave physical danger. The victim repeated her cringing, blood curdling cries for help a few further times, before the blue flashing lights of a police van, which sped up the adjacent road toward the aboriginal community, assured us that help was on the way. I slept uneasily from that point onward, for it was clear that something very violent had occurred only a kilometre or so from where we lay.

The next morning I was casually chatting to the park proprietor. After a while, I broached the subject of the nocturnal cries for help.

"Did you hear the screams last night?" I asked, still a bit wary from the experience.

"Screams?" he asked, genuinely vague.

"Yes," I replied. "I heard three awful screams at about 9 pm. The police were on the scene soon after that. Have you heard anything about what happened?"

"Oh, it's probably nothing," he replied, nonchalantly. "Just another kerfuffle from the aboriginal camp over the road."

Kerfuffle? By the chilling, piercing sound of those screams, a murder had been committed. Yet this bloke was dismissing the whole incident as a mere *kerfuffle*.

"We used to hear them three or four times a night, but there's only been a couple per week since the intervention," he added.

True to his prediction, we did indeed hear occasional screams, howls of pain or drunken fights as our nights in Mataranka rolled by. Each time, the police van would whiz past along the road, its blue light flashing against the night sky. An hour later, peace would settle over the fields, and we would all drop off to sleep. In time, I, too, started to dismiss the obvious violence as 'just another kerfuffle' - an attitude that had appalled me only a week earlier. Familiarity, for better or worse, breeds contempt.

The longer I stayed in Mataranka, the bigger fan I became of the interventionalist policies that had earlier offended my delicate sensibilities. We soon learned that the increased policing and the limits on alcohol purchases were having a positive effect on crime rate. In particular, the call outs to the nightly alcohol-fuelled violence at the indigenous camps had dropped markedly; the camp owner had not been exaggerating.

Despite the grumblings of the critics being true – the laws were clearly paternalistic, restrictive, and reeked of nanny state over-control – I could see their worth. If it took just a few extra minutes at the checkout, and a small loss of privacy, to prevent half a dozen bashings per week, then I was all for it. Manifestly, the safety of the vulnerable greatly outweighed the collateral loss of civil liberty. Hopefully the violence and crime rates in indigenous communities will continue to fall as the ratbags are weeded from such communities, and a different kind of normal takes its place.

The situation was similar in Katherine, which had recently banned all public consumption of alcohol. This hardline measure was in response to complaints that too many people, aborigines in particular, congregated on public land every day, doing little but sitting around drinking alcohol. Again, at first, this rule appeared to be a freedom-reducing, nanny state bow to racists. After all, our family and friends would often gather at parks for a barbeque or picnic, which, I am the first to admit, included goodly swigs of alcohol. On the other hand, we did not do this every day....

Nowhere in Australia is the uneasy relationship of our indigenous people to the bottle more clearly demonstrated than in the township of Halls Creek. Situated at the eastern end of the Kimberley, the town had an unenviable reputation as a cesspool of constant drunkenness. This accusation may sound a bit rich coming from a person with a declared interest in bourbon and beer, but a story - most claim it is true, but perhaps it is apocryphal –demonstrates the severity of Halls Creek's collective drinking problem.

In the 1980s, the government started using satellite imagery to monitor the outback for bushfires. This surveillance was undertaken because this area is so vast, and so sparsely populated, that often nobody noticed the fire had even begun until it had destroyed large tracts of lands. Suffice to say, this delayed bushfire detection is not a problem in, say, New York or Tokyo, but out here it was an issue for concern.

The early warning system depended upon infrared imaging, which detected the heat signals from the land. When the satellite detected a hot spot, it sent an alarm to the nearest fire brigade for investigation. The system had only just become active when it detected a large hot spot above Halls Creek. The local authorities were duly notified and rushed to attend the scene. Yet they could not find any bushfire; indeed, everything seemed as normal.

The satellite warning system was rechecked and re-calibrated, but again reported a large potential bushfire in the region of Halls Creek. Upon zeroing in upon the source, they traced the heat to the park in the middle of town, right across the road from the pub. Again, the local authorities investigated. Clearly, there was no fire.

It took some time before the boffins discovered the reason for the false positive signal. The answer was unfortunate and damning: the sun's rays were being reflected back up into space from the park, causing it to read as 'hot' on the satellite camera. What was causing the reflection?

Thousands of discarded, empty beer cans.

Before we started our journey, I failed to understand how Aboriginal people could disrespect their surroundings as such. Some camps in Broome were similarly filthy –torn blue tarps, discarded fast food wrappers, haphazard chicken wire, and empty beer bottles. The pile of rubbish at the entrance to the Cape Leveque peninsular could be seen from space. Why didn't the native residents simply clean up after themselves, for goodness sake?

I also wondered, with more than just a hint of racism, why their culture had never turned in any real way to farming, or other sustainable food production, such as animal husbandry. I was one of the voices who would have agreed with the complainants in Katherine; the sight of aboriginal groups lying around under trees all day in the public parks was, at least, an eyesore, and at worst, a public nuisance.

As our trip unfolded, my opinion gradually changed. I'm not saying I grew to *like* filthy rubbish piles or tawdry camps, nor did I become a paternal apologist for antisocial behaviour, but I think that I gained an inkling of the mind-set behind such behaviours. This shift occurred without me talking to anyone about the issues, or discussing these matters with indigenous people. The catalyst for this adjustment was, quite simply, the countryside itself.

If you had to describe the Australian outback in the Kimberley/Pilbara region in just three words, some of the main contenders would be *vast*, *barren* and *hot*. These adjectives are simple to read and readily imagined, yet until you live in these conditions for a few months, you do not fully appreciate them. I found that as the outback land slowly took a hypnotic hold over me, I came to appreciate a little more about its original inhabitants and their habits.

Most aborigines were nomadic. They had to be. Food was so scarce in this unforgiving environment that they had little option but to move onward, forever uncovering new sources of nourishment. Most of the time they simply discarded their rubbish into large heaps known as *middens*. It didn't matter if this pile became unsightly, because the tribe would soon be moving on. The space was so vast and unoccupied that neither they, nor anyone else, would encounter the detritus for hundreds, perhaps thousands, of years. This system was not irresponsible; it was, by far, the most efficient way to operate in this environment.

Unfortunately, archaeologists of the future are unlikely to look back upon a midden of empty beer cans with any reverence. Most aborigines, particularly those who live in townships, are no longer nomadic, so the rubbish just accumulates. However, in the same way that I claim that my Grandfather's Spanish heritage makes me partial to a siesta, olives and red wine, it would not surprise me if somewhere, deeply buried within indigenous DNA, is an inclination to simply toss rubbish aside as the most efficient way to operate.

Likewise, farming out here simply makes no sense. With the exception of the Ord Valley, near Kununurra, very few commercial crops are successfully grown in the outback. Animal husbandry? What would they raise? Kangaroos? Imagine the height of the fence that you would need to stop a 'big red' bounding its way to freedom. So again, I am guessing, admittedly without any anthropological research to back me up, or, in fact, without any basis other than my own hunch, that deep down, farming and other such long-term enterprises just do not appeal to the aboriginal psyche. 'Going walkabout' simply feels more right.

When you travel across this land, particularly in a car that has lost the benefit of air conditioning, you soon learn one habit: don't do *anything* that requires effort in the heat of the day. Since the 55 degree inferno of our bushwalk at Katherine Gorge, we had confined all of our exploring to the morning, or late afternoon. Heck, I even made sure I went to the toilet every day at 9 am, just so that I did not have to walk to the latrine in the middle of the day. The heat was just too sapping to contemplate any physical activity. Instead, we lay around, lazily, under trees, in the shade, simply waiting for the air to shed a few degrees. In short, we unconsciously mimicked the habits of the aboriginal groups in public parks that had so offended people. It took us just three months to adopt the lifestyle that our indigenous people had used for thousands of years.

It is clear that these habits do not neatly transfer into modern Australian towns, particularly when alcohol is introduced into the equation. Yet even though I do not necessarily condone such behaviours, a few months' travel through this vast, barren, hot, land endowed me with an appreciation of their genesis. A handful of understanding is a much easier load to carry than a mountain of disrespect.

I also came to realise, on a very gradual yet intimate level, why so much Aboriginal culture centres on the land. That red dirt really consumes you, and seeps into your bones without you realising; like Kimberley dust, which manages to creep into every part of you, (and even onto your toothbrush, inside your bag) so, too, does the essence of the land. It does not surprise me that the aboriginal fight for land rights is an issue that runs very deeply within them. I knew that I was going to miss those wide, red, open, hot, barren, godforsaken spaces when I arrived back home.

We spent the rest of our time in Matta – as in Kunna, a week's residence qualified me to use a diminutive – much as you would guess: reading, swimming, cooking, walking, and playing games with the kids. The campground's kindly owners also allowed me use of their office computer on which I re-created my tour notes as best I could; you would not be reading this rollicking tome were it not for their kind-heartedness. It also gave me a valid-sounding excuse to sit in their air conditioning for hours; pretending to read brochures in their waiting area was only good for an hour or so.

The boys and I also went fishing most days, but without further success. (Maybe Kath was right? *Naaaah*.) Nevertheless we enjoyed each other's company and took some bonding walks along the riverbank, ambling along in search of more productive fishing spots. Only once did I get a hit, but lost it. Yet the jolt of excitement that I felt was enough to let me know that the sport of barra fishing had completely hooked me.

After only a week, our car parts arrived from Melbourne. Our mechanic, Willie, had them fitted by lunch the next day, and we were on our way. We now had only eight days left of our holiday, and so, for the first time, reluctantly aimed for Brisbane. But of course, we managed to squeeze in a few final adventures along the way.

Chapter 16: Homeward Bound

After departing Mataranka, we headed south along the main highway. The first night of our homeward run we stopped at Daly Waters. You may have heard the expression "a one pub town". Daly Waters takes this concept further – the pub *is* the town. There is nothing else. No other businesses, no industry, no shops. Nothing. If you want something in Daly Waters –petrol, a postcard, dinner, marital aids, a combine harvester – then you "ask at the pub".

And a fine pub it was too. Generations of travellers had adorned the walls with all manner of bric-a-brac, from badges, business cards and bras, to caps, coins and cups. I added a simple business card to the collection. If you are ever in the neighbourhood, please drop in and let me know if it is still there. It is the fourth card down in the third column on the right hand side of the front bar panel.

The next day we headed south, turned left, and 850km later drove over the Queensland border. It almost felt like we were home already. Our stop that night was Camooweal. Don't go there. It was boring and characterless, and the pub had crappy food.

The next morning we took a quick detour to explore the Camooweal caves, which were apparently a spectacular 290 metres long and 70 metres deep. However, we eventually deduced that you have to descend into a very big deep dark hole to get in, which was impossible without semi-serious climbing gear. We left after a disappointing viewing of nothing but a big hole in the ground. Note to Queensland National Parks and the Camooweal council: have you heard of ladders? These big long holes in the ground could be a great tourist attraction for your area.

For the rest of the day we drove 750 km to Richmond. This neat outback town is the centre of dinosaur country. About 100 million years ago this region was underwater, but then someone pulled out the plug and the sea receded, leaving many marine dinosaurs trapped. As the water evaporated the animals died, sank and duly fossilised, leaving behind some of the most outstandingly complete fossils on earth. The local dinosaur museum housed real fossils, not casts or fakes.

The most impressive display was the *Pliosaur*. This fellow was found, covered by only a light dusting of dirt, by a local farmer. It lay on the ground in exactly the same position as it died all those millions of years ago. It was displayed in the museum in the same posture. This Pliosaur specimen is acknowledged internationally as one of the most compete dinosaur skeletons ever discovered.

I had been looking forward to a particular sporting event for a few weeks, so after lunch I ventured into a Richmond Pub to watch it on the bar's television. I greeted the barmaid with a friendly "Hi" while attempting to give her a country-boy type smile.

"I was wondering whether you were going to play the Norwegian Curling Championships Quarter Final on television today?" I asked.

"Err, I don't think so," she replied, looking at me quizzically, as if she had never heard of curling, or, more likely, Norway. "Perhaps try the other pub."

I thanked her for her brevity, and walked to the appropriately named Mud Hole Pub.

"Hi," I said to the barman, not bothering with the fake charm this time. "I was wondering whether or not you were going to play the Norwegian Curling Championships Quarter Final on television today?"

He looked at me with twisted eyebrows and a strange leer on his lips, leaving me in no doubt that he thought I was a weirdo.

"You want to watch curling? Really? When is it on?" he asked.

"Today at 2 pm," I replied.

"We didn't intend playing it," he said.

My spirits dropped – perhaps I wouldn't get to see the big game after all – but then the barman asked "Is it on Foxtel?"

"It's probably on mainstream TV," I replied.

Surely they knew that the curling was on this afternoon? I even expected that there would be a bit of a crowd to watch it with me, and create some atmosphere.

"I guess I could try to put it on," he added. "It's just that I've never had anyone ask to watch the Norwegian Curling Championships before."

He looked at the other weatherworn patrons sucking on their beers at the bar. His expression said: "I think this blow-in is some kind of poofter. What sort of wanker would watch the Norwegian Curling Championships?"

The bar flies directed a similar gaze at me. Nevertheless, the barman lazily flicked channels until he found the right one, and I settled in for an afternoon of sport watching. Everyone else returned to their beers and racing form guides, and did not once glance at the game that was completely capturing my attention.

Of course, it was not the Norwegian Curling Championships that I was watching. It was the AFL Grand Final – that's the Australian Football League, Australia's most popular code of anything, and the most watched programme on television every year since John Logie Baird was in diapers. The passage above is true, and represents exactly what happened – except, of course, you have to substitute "AFL footy grand final" for "the Norwegian Curling Championships Quarter Final". Read it again with that in mind and you'll understand how much of a stranger I felt.

I acknowledge that north-western Queensland is Rugby League country – a different type of footy, for those who are unaware of the distinction - but these blokes acted as if they had never even *heard* of Australian Rules Football. They certainly didn't know the Grand Final was on, and regarded me with great suspicion for wanting to watch it. It would be like living in the USA and not even knowing that the Superbowl was on. Nevertheless, Kath and the kids joined me in the Mud Hole at quarter time, and we spent the next two hours watching a decent game of footy.

The next day we motored across to the city of Townsville. An old mate of mine Bernie and his lovely wife Julie live there, so we dropped in to sponge off them for a couple of days. We cooked up the penultimate barra fillet for dinner, and then settled in for a long and satisfying drinking session. Although my wife is great company, I had spoken with very few other adults in three months, so I wasn't going to let this chance go to waste.

We covered lots of territory, and learned of news that we did not even know existed: the federal Liberal Party had a new leader, the world financial markets were in turmoil, and some football stars had been playing up. The more things change....

It was very late – about half past – when we eventually pulled up stumps. I awoke a few hours later feeling seedy and quickly realised my error. We had booked a Barrier Reef cruise for the day. The green feeling in my gills foretold that this wasn't going to be pleasant.

The green feeling was right. It wasn't long before the yawing motion of the boat amplified my hangover. After three hours of gradually escalating nausea, all the while lying to Kath and the kids that I felt fine, we finally reached our destination: the snorkelling and diving haven of Kelso Reef.

The whole family had soon donned diving gear, and was excitedly snorkelling amongst the coral. It was a delight to be back in the ocean. The kids had done plenty of snorkelling at Ningaloo so they took to the water like seasoned professionals. My hangover receded by the minute. Please bear with my superlatives when I say that the coral and aquatic life was vividly coloured, exceptionally beautiful and infinitely interesting.

Then I had a go at real scuba diving. It told the guide on the boat that I had already done "three or four dives" in my life in order to inflate my apparent experience. This was not a lie but it stretched the truth, as all dives had been on the same weekend about two decades previously. I told this fib so that I could accelerate through the boring training stage, and explore the reef sooner. I'd be fine. How hard could it be?

By the time we had descended to the 12-metre mark, I was seriously regretting my little white lie. I felt desperately anxious, and had an overwhelming urge to return to the surface and take a breath of real air. It just felt unnatural to stay underwater for so long. A feeling that the regulator would slip out of my mouth just would not leave me alone. I spent the next few minutes meditating away the panic, all the while giving the guide the "thumbs-up" signal to inform him that I was doing great. Eventually, by a combination of relaxing, meditating and distracting myself, I was able to swim without panic, and almost (but not quite) managed to enjoy the last five minutes. But I refused to let go of the regulator lest it fall out of my mouth.

I'd love to Scuba dive again, but next time I think I'll start a little more gradually. Maybe I'll even submit myself to the half-hour orientation lesson before I don the gear.

The next day we drove about 600km to a free coastal camp, where we had one last stroll on the muddy beach and a final evening campfire. As the fire embers were dying away, so too was our journey.

And so the next day we turned directly for home. The sky had some strange whitish-grey objects floating in it that I distantly recalled. What were they called again? Ah, that's right, clouds. We hadn't seen any since Denham, over two months previously. The landscape also changed. Fruit trees and farmland steadily gave way to billboards and buildings, and before we knew it we were stuck in the traffic on Brisbane's Gateway Bridge.

I tried the Outback Motorist's Gidday Wave as we drove down Wynnum Road, but nobody waved back. Welcome home.

*

For the record, the tally of our car problems was:

- A blown engine (two weeks in Kununurra)
- A dud clutch and starter motor (a further week in Kununurra)
- Broken air conditioner and exhaust sensor (one day in Darwin)
- Blown radiator (two more days in Darwin)
- Dead stereo and air conditioner (one day in Katherine)

- Buggered wheel bearings and air conditioner compressor (eight days in Mataranka).

Despite this long list, please don't think that our mechanical woes detracted from our holiday. The places in which we were stuck – Kununurra, Darwin and Mataranka – were all great fun. The down time presented us with the opportunity – nay, compelled us - to relax. Pertinently, I might not have caught any barra if the car had not broken down (twice). As an added bonus, I can now locate the air intake on the Jackaroo, and can identify more parts than just the thermostat.

There are worse things than car problems that can happen to you out there. Remember the helicopter flight that crashed over the Bungles, killing the pilot and all three passengers. Now *that* would have ruined our holiday.

Take my advice: go and see outback Australia. You won't regret it. Just tow a spare car behind you for parts.

And yes, no matter where or when you're reading this, I'm *still* smiling over that barra.

The End

More books by John Perrier
from JP Publishing Australia

"Back Pain: How to get rid of it Forever"
- Self help/back pain/self treatment
- Adult/Young Adult readers
- Available as print edition or two-volume E-Book

"Captain Rum – A Wondrous Adventure"
Edited by Prof. H.D. (Bert) Lampluck
- Historical Fiction/Maritime adventure
- Adult/Young Adult readers
- Published by JP Publishing Australia
- Available as print or E-Book

"A Few Quiet Beers with God"
- Science-fiction/comedy
- Young Adult/Teen/Young-at-heart adults
- Available as print or E-Book

"Using Your Brain to Get Rid of Your Pain"
A simple, common sense guide on how to manage stress, reduce pain, and think more healthily.
- Self help/healthy living
- Adult/Young adult
- Available as print or E-Book

You can find more online at
www.JPpublishingAUSTRALIA.com

"Back Pain: How to Get Rid of it Forever"

The title says it all: this book will help you permanently banish your back pain. In three logical sections, it shows you how to feel better.

The first section makes it easy for you to understand your back pain. Using simple, clear language, it explains the structure of your spine, and demystifies many common pain-provoking conditions. The second part offers a unique quiz that will help you to classify your injury into one of four types. In this way, you will learn how to cure your pain, not someone else's.

In part three, the advice flows thick and fast. You will learn clever techniques that will help you to use your spine more efficiently, and discover how to think, eat, relax, and sleep away your pain. You'll also find useful information on exercises, x-rays, medication and muscles, plus some tips on how to choose a spinal health practitioner. Of course, all of the advice will be tailored to your specific problem.

Because the cure uses well-proven techniques, your relief won't just last a few days or weeks. You will feel better *forever*.

*

"The best self help back book I have ever read."

Dr Keith Charlton, Chiropractor, former governor of the Australian Spinal Research Foundation.

More information on Back Pain can also be found at
www.physioworks.com.au

"Captain Rum: A Wondrous Adventure"
Edited by Prof. H.D. (Bert) Lampluck

When an Oxford Professor stumbles upon an old naval Captain's log, he unwittingly discovers what many scholars now agree is one of the greatest maritime adventures in history.

In 1821, Captain Fintan McAdam set sail from London, solo, in search of adventure. During his journey he discovered incredible new worlds, and interacted with their amazing inhabitants. McAdam's voyage also forced him to confront his enemies within, learning much about himself.

Captain Rum, as told in McAdam's own words through his journal, is a tale of discovery, despair and delight. It will keep you enthralled through many a stormy night.

"A Few Quiet Beers with God"

Set in Australia in the year 2031, this story is science-fiction comedy at its best.

When Dave, a hopeless but lovable 34 year old, meets Alexandra, the girl of his dreams, he feels as though his luck has finally changed. But due to his ineptness with technology, he tragically loses contact with her.

Meanwhile, the lust for supremacy of two powerful Americans ignites a bitter feud. Their fight reaches around the globe and soon entwines not only Dave and Alexandra, but also a superstar football player nicknamed 'God'.

Their final meeting precipitates an event that no-one saw coming.

"Using Your Brain to get Rid of Your Pain"

A simple, common sense guide on how to manage stress, reduce pain, and think more healthily.

This book will help you to *feel better*. You'll not only learn how to reduce or cure your aches and pains, but you'll discover techniques that will help you to relax away the stresses and strains of everyday life.

However, this book does not contain masses of complex psychiatry, nor is it a collection of old wives' remedies. You won't have to use any drugs to achieve amazing results, nor will you be required to burn incense or wear mystical healing crystals in an ankle bracelet.

Instead, you will learn how to relieve your pain using the most natural cures known to medical science. Furthermore, the treatment will have beneficial spin-offs rather than unpleasant or dangerous side effects. Better still, it won't cost you a single penny!

INCLUDES COMPLIMENTARY AUDIO TRACK!
See www.JPpublishingAUSTRALIA.com for details

What other health professionals have said...
"This is an easy-to-understand guide to stress and its related symptoms. The author explains these sometimes difficult concepts by using simple, relevant examples, and enlivens the discussion with a touch of humour along the way. Most importantly, it shows you in simple terms how to manage your own problems. I heartily recommend this book to all sufferers of chronic pain." *Ian McKenzie, Clinical Psychologist*

Connect and Contact

Your comments, criticisms, typos, praise, offers for movie deals, and suggestions are all very welcome. Please contact us by any of the methods below.

Email:
JDPpublishingAUSTRALIA@gmail.com
(please note the extra 'D')

Facebook:
https://www.facebook.com/JPpublishingAustralia

Website:
www.JPpublishingAUSTRALIA.com

Mail:
JP Publishing Australia
56 Quirinal Crescent
Seven Hills, Brisbane
AUSTRALIA   4170

15428903R00126

Printed in Great Britain
by Amazon